Penguin Handbooks

Help Your Child to Read and Write, and More

David Mackay grew up in the Orkney Islands. At the age of sixteen he
went to London and after the war he became a teacher. In 1964 he
joined the Nuffield Programme in Linguistics and English Teaching at
University College, London.

He left London in 1973 and went to work in the Dutch West Indies,
where he is at present concerned with the renewal of the curriculum in
three small English-speaking Caribbean islands. He has two daughters,
both of whom are teachers, and is a proud grandfather. He is the
compiler of *A Flock of Words*, a volume of poetry for young children.

Joseph Simo was born in Barcelona in 1945. He studied law at
Barcelona University and then went to Paris for several years, where
he studied political science and philosophy and gained an M.A. in
Sociology and a Ph. D. in Philosophy. He then embarked on private
research in linguistics at the London School of Economics Library and the
Centre for Language in Primary Education. He has carried out fieldwork
for the Bernard van Leer Foundation and worked with David Mackay
in the Dutch West Indies. He now lives in New York where he is
carrying out research work in curriculum development and training as
a psychoanalyst.

David Mackay and Joseph Simo

Help Your Child to Read and Write, and More

Penguin Books

Penguin Books Ltd,
Harmondsworth, Middlesex, England
Penguin Books Inc.,
7110 Ambassador Road, Baltimore, Maryland 21207, U.S.A.
Penguin Books Australia Ltd,
Ringwood, Victoria, Australia
Penguin Books Canada Ltd,
41 Steelcase Road West, Markham, Ontario, Canada
Penguin Books (N.Z.) Ltd,
182–190 Wairau Road, Auckland 10, New Zealand

First published 1976
Copyright © David Mackay and Joseph Simo, 1976

Made and printed in Great Britain by
Hazell Watson & Viney Ltd, Aylesbury, Bucks
Set in Monotype Times

For Nigel, Stephen, Patrick, Diane, Beth, Esther,
Sergi, Xavier, Sarah and all the children
who still teach us so much

Contents

Acknowledgements

Many people have helped us, directly and indirectly, in writing this book: teachers and children, linguists, sociologists, children's librarians, students of early childhood education. In particular we are grateful to Mrs Kate Austen of Kingsgate Infant School, London; Mrs Philips of Robensfield Nursery School, London; Mrs Day of John Milton Primary School; and Miss M. Sykes of Berry Brow C.P. School, Huddersfield; to Professor M. A. K. Halliday for his personal help and advice and for allowing us to use part of his study of Nigel and who, with Professor Basil Bernstein, contributed to our understanding of children as environmental learners; to Mr K. Albrow for sharing his insight into the nature of English orthography; to Mrs Griselda Barton for her enthusiastic guidance in selecting children's books; to BBC Radio London for permission to quote extensively from an interview on children's play; and finally to Patrick for permission to use his manuscript of Roy the Boy, and to his parents for information about the way he wrote his stories at home.

Introduction

In the following pages we call young children 'prodigious learners'. We are not thinking of the kind of learning associated with school. For during their first five years before children go to school they have been engrossed in extensive learning, starting with only a *potential* to learn. This is a time when children especially depend on the human, social and cultural environment into which they are born. That is, they depend on the place, the people, the objects and the activities of which their environment consists, for opportunities to learn in a great variety of play-like activities. The ways in which parents support these, both by the quality of their affection and companionship and by what they provide for their children, are of fundamental importance to how successful children will be in the very different learning situations with which school confronts them.

Gradually it is coming to be recognized that the pre-school years are among the most formative in every child's life – that on these early years his future development into adulthood mainly depends. But still the tremendous learning potential all children have is seldom realized to the full.

These are some of the reasons why our book begins with the way young children develop as 'environmental learners'. We are concerned to show the serious intent with which children take up the many learning tasks that confront them. At home, the 'teachers' of a pre-school child have no training in how to teach. This has advantages and disadvantages: it has advantages when they are prepared to follow the interests of a child and lead him into a greater share of their own; it has disadvantages when they teach *what* the child ought to know and *how* he ought to know it by recollecting their own school experiences.

To clarify this important issue, the first part of our book deals with the development of young children with particular concern for the

ways in which language development takes place. This may appear
to be a long way from reading and writing. We try to show on what
reading and writing depend and how this can develop naturally out
of the child's desire to do, to understand, to know about everything
around him. We might as easily have shown how the same is true for
mathematics, science or music.

In the second part of our book we have given what we consider to
be a good example of 'natural' learning in one child and of the way
her parents provided for this by learning from their daughter as well
as by helping her to teach herself.

Because we know the fear many people have that their children
will not read and write well enough, we suggest things they can do for
their children. Helping their children read and write is something they
can and should do. If they do so in a way which permits a child to
continue learning through play activities, through self-made discovery
in a helpful environment, there need be no fear of not knowing what
to do, and how and when to do it.

Each child has to find his own way of acquiring and relating the
complex skills that we label reading and writing. The second part of
our book also sets out in detail (some of which is technical and intended as reference material) something of what children have to
learn. We do not say exactly how they will do this, for there is not
only one correct way, *only* one correct time. Our strong advice to
parents, family friends, teachers and students, is that they should let
each learner guide them in the ways they might offer to help.

Behind Diane who is shown discovering reading and writing and
Patrick who is already an accomplished hand, lie a great deal of
informal teaching and freedom to learn. We believe that many more
children, if they are supported properly in the early years, can learn
prodigiously – and not just in reading and writing, but in much more.

1   Children as Environmental Learners

Some of the most difficult questions concerning children are those dealing with their learning: What do children need to learn? What do they learn? How do they learn? Children must learn to live and communicate within the social structure. Thus, learning his mother tongue is one of the most remarkable tasks every child undertakes, so questions about language acquisition and development are of special importance.

What is it like to have no language? How do children learn to speak? How do they learn to read and write? How best can we help them to learn? These questions cannot be answered at all fully, but we start with them because they are essential to understanding how children develop their intellectual potential. Little is yet known about this, although the acquisition and development of language in children have become established parts of child studies. But enough is known for it to be no longer excusable to make simplistic statements like 'they've either got it or they haven't', or 'everything is inside their heads'. For there is nothing inside their heads beyond a brain, structured in such a way that the child can recognize what is going on around him and gives him the ability to build a series of statements about the world. The brain gives the child the potential to understand and master the outside world, his environment.

A child goes through many stages in the course of his intellectual growth.

Before his language emerges he will develop successively perception, identification and recognition. Repeated perceptions of objects, such as trees, under many different circumstances, lead to his identifying and recognizing trees as a distinct category of object, things with a quality of their own and quite different from other objects. In the next stage the category is not only recognized but named 'tree'. This is the stage at which language emerges. The child does this spontaneously within his actual environment, from what is around him, and available to him, if properly encouraged.

Each child is an individual and learns in his own way, in his own time and from his own environment. These three aspects of learning are inseparable, and it is misleading to consider them as independent and isolated from each other; they are given a certain autonomy here only to make the concepts clearer.

By 'own way' of learning we mean that the child has considerable freedom in what he learns about and how he learns about it; he can investigate what interests him at a certain moment. By 'own time' we mean that there is no fixed chronological pattern of learning; as Piaget has shown, learning progresses in stages, but the age at which a child moves from one stage to another is not fixed.* The link between 'own way' and 'own time' is clear: what the child finds out in his way at one stage enables him to go on to the next, more complex stage, and so decides the time at which he is ready to do this. It is possible, though difficult, for the process to be accelerated. It is also possible, and all too easy, for it to be delayed.

The child's way and time to a certain extent depend on his own 'natural' abilities, but they are also very dependent on his environment. His learning is limited by what is available to him, so the environment largely determines the way and time, as well as the content, of his learning.

The child's environment is not just a physical world; it is a social world, full of human beings. The child lives in a human group, usually a family, which provides for his physical needs: food, shelter, affection, security and so on. He also learns language and interaction rituals from them, and puts together a whole network of social meanings which make up what the world is for him.

Society is not a homogeneous unit; it is a maze of cultures co-existing in the shadow of a dominant culture. Consequently children growing up in different cultural environments follow different patterns of cognitive, emotional and linguistic development. There is, for instance, no universal 'standard English'; each child grows up

---

*Piaget's work is fundamental to understanding human learning, and many popular accounts of his work now exist. See M. Brearly and E. Hitchfield, *A Teacher's Guide to Reading Piaget*, Routledge & Kegan Paul, London 1967: Schocken, New York, 1967.

speaking a *dialect*, in the sense of a particular form of English spoken by those in his environment. The dialect will have its own patterns of linguistic interaction and distinctive linguistic features, such as phonological, lexico-grammatical and semantic structures. The child's cultural environment takes in beliefs and attitudes, values which will direct his judgements, roles he will be rehearsed in, expectations which will signal the direction his development will take. Each child, then, receives an *environmental heritage*, a set of characteristic environmental features, physical and social, which constitute the material he uses to build his identity as a human and social being.

The child is not enclosed once and for all in the same environment; there is *environmental mobility*. His development initially depends on his environmental heritage but he will later move from his own environment into another. For many children this move takes place when they begin school. A child may find it easy to enter this new, more formal environment, or, as often happens, may clash with it. This conflict is usually most severe at a linguistic and conceptual level; the school uses the levels of the dominant culture and excludes the others, so he may not understand what is asked of him and may not be able to perform in a certain way. He may find it easier to adjust to the external behaviour asked of him, like sitting down and being quiet.

This emphasis on the major role of environment in a child's development contradicts some well-established social ideologies and myths spread by the dominant culture to mask its domination. It opposes the ideas that 'everyone gets what he deserves' and 'he who works hard succeeds in life'. Many young children start off in a cultural framework different from the dominant one; when they enter another environment, the school, modelled on the structures of the dominant culture, they do badly because it is foreign to them. This does not mean that these children start with a 'social handicap' but that the actual socio-cultural structures simply penalize them for not being part of the dominant culture. To use a metaphor, it is like putting an atheist into a monastery and expecting him to adapt his behaviour immediately and do well as a monk. It also opposes those views which presuppose that the only correct pattern of development is that of the middle-class child; those who do not follow that pattern are often thought 'lacking' and labelled inadequate.

Emphasis on environment also reduces the importance of concepts like intelligence and heredity. A child who is unable to cope in school with concepts and language quite different from those in his own cultural environment may be called 'stupid'; his 'stupidity' may then be related to his 'stupid' parents. These attitudes display enormous prejudice and ignorance, but unfortunately they are still to be found among many teachers.

Since there is no 'correct' and universal pattern of child development 'intelligence' tests are fair only to the children coming from the dominant environment. Children from environments with other patterns of development are immediately at a disadvantage. American research shows that the Intelligence Quotient (I.Q.) of a child living in a very favourable environment, compared with that of a child living in an unfavoured environment, increases by 2·5 points per year for the first four years of life. In France Colette Chiland measured the I.Q.s of children entering school at six years of age and the I.Q.s of the same children five years later. Those from favourable socio-cultural environments, that is, the ones better fitted at the beginning, increased their I.Q.s. Of those from 'lower', socio-cultural environments not one had increased his I.Q., and three of those who had scored 110 at the age of six scored lower five years later.

This does not mean that children with lower scores are in fact less intelligent than those with the higher scores. Up to now most intelligence tests have suited only those children in whose image they have been designed – the children from favoured socio-cultural environments. They therefore under-rate the abilities of all children who do not fit this pre-established model, stigmatizing in particular those from unfavourable environments. The low scores achieved by children from unfavoured environments are used to justify educational systems rather than expose their weaknesses, although teachers could be and should be aware of the importance of environment.

Teachers can actually increase the disparities, because children who are valued as 'intelligent' are helped and encouraged in ways which are withheld from the less highly valued children. An interesting experiment illustrates the point neatly. Professor Rosenthal gave his psychology students two groups of rats. One group was said to contain 'very clever' rats, the other 'stupid' rats. In fact they had been chosen randomly, and they were only divided into groups to suggest to the students that there was a real difference in intelligence between them. Both groups of rats were put through standard tests. The first group – which the students believed were clever, got far better results than the second, which the students believed were stupid. Rosenthal* then carried out an equivalent experiment in eighteen classes of a primary school. Teachers were told that certain pupils had had particularly brilliant results in a (non-existent) intelligence test. Again they had in fact been chosen randomly. In a year the pupils whom teachers expected to be 'very clever' increased their I.Q.s much more than those expected to be less clever. The attitudes of the students to the rats and the teachers to the pupils were decisive in their effect on the performance of the rats and the children. The teachers gave more and better attention to the children they believed were clever and this accounted for the dramatic increase in their I.Q.s.

So, environmental features are of the greatest importance to the child, and fundamental to an understanding of how children learn. Parents and immediate family make up the major part of the child's social environment and their attitudes are crucial. We begin the book with this important point, which will be developed as we look at the ways in which parents contribute to the development of language in their children.

*R. Rosenthal and L. Jacobson, *Pygmalion in the Classroom: Teacher Expectation and Pupils' Intellectual Development*, Holt, Rinehart & Winston, London and New York, 1968.

2   Playing and Learning

Often we refer to children as 'prodigious learners' with a pleasant feeling of astonishment at how much they learn in a short time. However, they are also sometimes prodigiously *frustrated* people. For many children have not only learned very little but have been filled with fear, confusion and a vague sense of 'not being good', a feeling of 'good for nothing'.

At birth each child enters a world which is entirely strange to him. Superficially his environment is the same as that of everyone around him. But to him it is foreign in all respects – even the people in it are unknown to him. Nothing of their familiarity with it and with one another is his. He has to begin discovering a foreign territory and its inhabitants; all through the first years of his life he will be an 'explorer'. In a remarkably short time though he will begin to find things out, to experiment, to inquire, to tell, to describe, to speculate and to wonder. He has no alternative; understanding his environment is a major necessity. But he cannot do this on his own. He must have the help of people and objects around him.

To learn how to do this needs many opportunities for talking to adults. If children have this they can make do with everyday materials to realize their imagining and work out their experiments. Most of a child's experiments, inquiries and speculations may be labelled 'play'. Serious misunderstanding of the nature of play in young children often arises because it looks extremely simple. Adults have usually forgotten their own childhood experiences and fail to understand what children must learn about the ways in which their bodies work; about their feelings and those of other people; about why people behave as they do; about sharing and competing; about exploring objects and relationships between sets of objects; about the nature of the real world. The word 'play' refers to the way children come to terms with knowing, feeling and moving and if they are allowed, children will do what they are able to do. But they will be hampered by dismissive adult attitudes to play. Play is a serious business for each child and one he is engaged in for no reward other than the value derived from what he is doing.

So far it is not so difficult: *talking* and *being talked to* and *everyday materials*. Children also need freedom from endless noes and don'ts, from endless commands and charges: 'Don't do that,' 'Sit quietly,' 'Stop that', 'If you make a mess I'll smack you.' They need warmth and a place for working that is not going to fill them with the fear of accidents, damage and mess. The three great blocks to learning are:

(1) fear of what adults think and expect;
(2) confusion about what they are supposed to be doing or what they may and may not do; and
(3) (after the adults around them have constructed their Does and Dont's) boredom because there is nothing worthwhile left for them to do or because they have lost the desire to do anything. Children are not by nature lazy any more than adults are – although they may become so if the wrong things are constantly demanded of them.

The space children need in order to understand their environment will be dictated by each particular stage of development and by the learning appropriate to this. They need space for moving, for running and jumping and climbing. They need to be close to an adult for listening to a story and looking at pictures and talking. They need uncramped space while making things and experimenting: a table-top, a space on the floor, a draining-board and things for water play, a space for working with clay and paints. Then they need a different kind of space for clean work with paper and coloured pens. They need the wide space outside for making discoveries about sights and sounds and objects, and a small, private place to keep treasures – stones, shells, feathers, match boxes, stamps and all those objects that have special significances for them. They also need a few simple tools: brushes, round-nosed scissors, paste, sellotape, bright paints, crayons, chalks; and a few materials: paper, bits of wood, nails, odds and ends of wool, coloured wrappings, string, an old magnet, a small mirror, glass beads, bricks and boxes and cartons of all sorts and sizes. They specially need someone who cares about their doings without violating their privacy; someone who is ready to guide, to suggest and to praise at the right moment without dictating what is going to be done; someone who is 'always there' without being a guard on duty. This 'someone' is not only the mother but whoever is a part of the child's environment. In a programme on BBC Radio London Mrs Chrissy Channel described the way in which she provided things for her children to do. The influence of playgroups on her thinking is very clear; but her understanding of how to give her children interesting activities at home is her own remarkable contribution to their upbringing. As she herself remarks, 'you've got to think of them more than you've got to think of the mess'. She accepts her children's needs seriously and ensures that home is a place for the whole family to share and use in their own ways. She says nothing of the extra work this entails because it is clear she considers this a natural part of her adult role. She takes some care to give them suitable materials to play with. She appreciates *what* children like to play with and *how* they play. She refrains from stereotyped reactions about what children ought to do and the roles they must take in their play: 'Even boys – you find that they like dolls . . . I always had a couple of dolls upstairs that they could wash . . .'

For Chrissy's children there is no feeling of boredom and frustration. And what is most important, their chance to talk and discuss is enhanced by their mother's interest in what they are doing. 'If they find something that occupies them for a long time it makes me happy and them happy as well.' This does not mean that in order to keep them occupied you need to give them everything, that they must 'own' the whole house or flat and those living in it. 'When we moved in we had three bedrooms. We had one, the children had another one, so there was one empty and that was just sort of a rubbish room. That was the only room that really got messed up. They didn't sort of wander in from it to the other rooms a lot.'

INTERVIEWER: 'What about things that are messy like painting and so on. Where do you get the paints from?'

MRS CHANNEL: 'Well, when he was little, he just used to use the paints in the tin. But now through the Playgroup I've learned that you can buy tins of powder paint, which is better. It's the same as the paper – any paper will do – you know, children are not fussy. They don't really like anything expensive. The same as the big brushes which are better for the children. It's better really if you've got a blackboard you could attach the paper to, which is easier for the child to sort of squiggle. They like all that freedom with their arms. I think that works out better and if you put a big sheet of polythene on the floor then it won't cause a lot of mess. They like pasting. They'd cut some shapes out of paper and stick them on to other pieces of paper. They like cutting things out of material, although sometimes when they're little you have to cut the shapes out for them (it's hard for them to cut material) and they'd stick them on the paper. You can buy rounded scissors that are not sharp at all but they're sharp enough for paper. They do cut paper.

'The other thing they like is the dough. I never realized that dough can be so thrilling; and the powder paint you buy you can mix with the dough, it's marvellous because it's colourful. They really want to do this and it does occupy a lot of time, you know, and that's all children have, time, isn't it? They had bowls of water. They played with their boats in the water or they played with sieves . . ., or bottles that they can fill up and pour out again. I found that they enjoyed that a lot. Sponges, anything, old Fairy Liquid bottles, anything like that.'

INTERVIEWER: 'You didn't find that made a big mess playing with water?'

MRS CHANNEL: 'Well I put sheets of polythene down. It soon mops up and when you're sort of restricted like that you've got to think of them more than you've got to think of the mess.'

What will children learn from all this? They learn to discover the properties of everything, to feel everything, to try everything out, exercising skills and mastering techniques. Their practice of many different skills is not so as to do things better than someone else, but just to do things better than they did before, for they 'know' better than before. There is great personal satisfaction to be had from such attitudes to work. They do not have to produce anything like a factory hand or an office clerk. Indeed they may only discover what they are making while they are doing something else. What they end up with may often be different from the ideas and intentions they started with, provided they have freedom to make personal decisions. They do more than master skills: they learn to solve problems with careful thought and imagination. They discover facts and they build theories about how things are. They extend their ability to feel and to express feelings.

In all this learning adults play several parts: they see that all is well; they help when difficulties arise; and more important, they are able to make proposals and lead children to discover something entirely new. Educational guidance with very young children is at best a simple, truthful, spontaneous reaction to children's needs. To be most helpful to children adults should be able to take pleasure in children's company, to listen to them, to participate when they are needed, to make all kinds of opportunities available and to enjoy these activities with children. What they need to do most of all is to spare time and trouble to be with children; to accompany them as far as they are able into the extending world of childhood, to understand as much of this as they are able to and to respect and encourage children in the activities they undertake.

There is no better way to turn childhood into an arid desert than to sit well-fed, well-clothed children in a corner and ignore them 'until they're interesting'. As one mother put it: 'Well, she can't talk yet, can she? Oh, I'll talk to her – when she can talk.' Another mother complained: 'Chatter, chatter, chatter, that's all you ever do. Do you think I have nothing better to do than listen to you all day? Now shut up!' Children who are forced into silence and inactivity through such attitudes are in great danger though they may give every appearance of physical well-being. Ignorance of the child's need to talk with adults and to play with other children as well as on his own may rob him of the most powerful influence in his whole education.

Thus, playing means being creative, using the whole personality in the individual's way to the discovery of the self. It is sometimes believed by those who have had too little opportunity to play or too restricted a form of play, that creativity – as well as intelligence – is a 'gift' of Nature. Maybe this would be so if we considered Nature to mean basically 'social quality' and thus environment. We do not consider that kind of creativity to be the 'making of geniuses'. Something more than a creative environment is needed for a Picasso or a Joyce to flourish and there is no such thing as a make-yourself-a-genius recipe. The creativity we are considering here is the involvement of the whole personality in the child's search for an identity.

Exploration of the environment and search for an identity can be seen as the main purposes of play, and these are matters which concern each individual and the children they care for. These purposes of play can be encouraged or dismissed by the child's environment. Thus, the outcome of the child's inquiries – his level of creativity and discovery – can generally be accounted for by the environment in which he lives.

Indeed it is a very different thing to be born into a family with parents working till late, with not much time to spare and – even with the best of the intentions – not knowing where to find suitable guidance materials, than to be born in the 'good' bourgeois family. This does not mean that we think the 'bourgeois family' is the most suitable pattern of growth and development. Far from it. Indeed we want to stress, in order to prevent false conclusions being drawn, the fact that the quality of the child's play does *not* depend on the income his family has; for play has nothing to do with expensive toys but everything to do with an *attitude* towards the child's needs. Needs which can be met successfully by everybody if an attitude like Mrs Channel's is taken.

In his play the child will have, in addition to the expectations placed upon his playing, the materials which will be given to him; the space given to him, the does and don'ts given to him. From the beginning, a child must have as clear as possible an idea of what his play space is and which are his play materials. He should be allowed to investigate *what interests him* and he should have the opportunity of choosing from a variety of possibilities. If his creativity and inquiries are allowed and encouraged they are more likely to become constructive than destructive or messy – any mess he may make early on is only due to lack of skill in handling materials, and it is essential for him to practise the skills he is trying to master. Destructive feelings are more likely to arise in frustrated, repressed children. If such feelings appear in a child's behaviour, instead of blaming his 'barbaric' feelings and trying to correct him it would be better to revise his environment, to try to 'correct' the environment.

Of course 'what interests him' must not include any object which will harm him. A plastic mug, a smooth stick, large coloured beads, a clean paper bag, such are the things from which he can make many discoveries. He will for instance learn that a plastic mug can contain liquid and also certain solids; he must learn how to hold it; he must learn what happens if it is turned upside down; he must learn how it balances, how it rolls; he must learn about its roundness, its shape, its relative size, how it feels to his mouth.

Obviously dangerous objects or substances *must* be kept out of reach of children. At the same time, they *should* be allowed to know about their properties. If a child is interested in a knife, for instance, he should be taught how to use a blunt one.

The *first stage* in the child's play is that in which he discovers the properties of objects surrounding him. Once this has been completed he will learn how to use these objects, make them play a diversity of roles. These play objects are usually known as *toys*. Toys can be either objects especially manufactured and sold for children to play with, or *any* object – boxes, old scrap materials, etc. – that children use in their play.

Play, Toys and Play Materials

Too often play is regarded only as a means of keeping children quiet and out of the way. The best that can be said is that this is an unfortunate view for it supposes that play is an activity *without* any pedagogical value. We think – with Dr Winnicott – that 'it is in playing and only in playing that the individual child or adult is able to be creative and to use the whole personality, and it is only in being creative that the individual discovers the self.'*

In our societies, manufactured toys often have a socio-economic value that the 'objects' children play with do not have. Such toys are often *not* an object for the child to play with but a 'present' given on special occasions determined by society's values: many people buy toys only at Christmas even though children play all year round. What is even more strange is that the reasons which guide the choice of bought toys often have no connection whatsoever with the child's world and with his needs, being the parents' response to toy advertisements and toy 'fashions' displayed in the windows of big stores. There may also be an element of 'social class display': 'I must get

*D. W. Winnicott, *Playing and Reality*, Pelican, Harmondsworth, 1974, p. 63.

the *best* for my children, no matter what the price.' The best, as far as toys are concerned, are *not* necessarily the most expensive nor the most sophisticated.

Clock-work soldiers, walkie-talkie dolls, mechanical cars etc. do of course have a certain fascination for children (and sometimes as much for adults) but the interest doesn't last long. A question anyone should ask himself before buying a toy is: 'Who am I buying this toy for – the child or myself?' It can be argued that adults usually do not buy toys to play with themselves. Maybe not, but perhaps for some personal 'prestige' reasons or because certain technology which is out of the child's understanding and interest fascinates them. Another question people should ask themselves before buying toys is: 'What kind of *values* do they incorporate?' It is very important to ask this question when one sees that guns, machine-guns and the like – 'toys' directed to mimic war, murder, killing and human destruction – are persistent 'best-sellers'.

Finally, if bought toys are the only toys a child has, he will learn from a very early age to be a passive *consumer*. The skills he could have developed by being the *producer* of some of his toys are stopped right at the beginning by the vicious cycle of buy, use quickly, waste and buy again. The following example illustrates the escape from 'consumer' tactics.

Beth is a delightful six-year-old girl who can be described as a *player*. She spends most of her time creating play situations in which she involves many toys as well as anyone who is interested. Although her parents are professionals with no great economic problems, most of Beth's toys are home-made. There are regular sessions of toy-making in the house. Beth's father, a skilful designer, provides her with a doll's house, and doll's furniture as well as puzzles and constructional items made of cardboard or plywood. At the age of six Beth is herself able to make most of her dolls, puppets and animals and even a funny-looking 'school-house'. Only occasionally does she ask for technical help from either her mother or her father. Not only does she put a great deal of energy into playing but she has already mastered a wide range of manual skills as well as a great ability for combining colours, materials and textures in the making of her toys. When we gave Beth a lovely hand-made South American doll, she made a careful 'study' of how it was made and finally said: 'She's beautiful. I'll *make* a friend for her . . . she doesn't like to be alone . . .'

The most suitable toys for children are often the sort that will become whatever the child's imagination commands. Empty cardboard boxes can become ambulances, trains, boats, castles or horses. They are also cheap and disposable. It is even better if these toys can be 'dignified' by a little paint and some additional details to make them more 'visual'. Given space to create make-believe situations and a freedom from adult pestering about tidiness, about 'not cluttering the room up with your old rubbish', children will invent one situation after another for long concentrated periods of time. They become immersed in exploring new ideas for changing ordinary objects into whatever their inner images require. They talk to themselves all the while and in this way fuse ideas and objects into continuously changing patterns of play.

The contribution of play in the child's language development is very important. Children seldom play silently – even when playing on their own. They are constantly 'rehearsing' their language.

They need language as well as objects to create play situations. They recreate real situations in order to understand their significance and their meaning. Imagining and reality fuse in new ways to permit children to discover some aspect of life around them. Thus while talking to dolls, or driving in a cardboard-box 'car' or playing trains, they will comment on, speculate about and describe aspects of an incident they are making up; they will ask questions and answer them. All this they may well do on their own as well as with adults and other children. But however they set up the play situation, it is language which forms and shapes it. It is while they are experimenting in this way that they are learning to master the functions of language and the meanings that reach them from the people around them. It is not by accident that children who are 'great talkers' are usually 'great players', and silent children are those who have been deprived of play in one way or another.

Well-made and well-designed 'commercial' toys do exist with a quality of versatility which allows children to use them as their play dictates. The better toy manufacturers have designed toys to support children's learning.

Books on Play and Preschool Education

E. GWENDA BARTRAM, *Not Yet Five*, Charles Crest, Croydon, 1972.

A brief guide to activities which will help children's intellectual development and prepare them for school.

EDUCATIONAL TESTING SERVICE (edited by Henry Chauncey, introduction by Urie Bronfenbrenner), *Soviet Pre-School Education, Volume 1: Program of Instruction, Volume 2: Teacher's Commentary*, Holt, Rinehart & Winston, London and New York, 1969.

The value system and the behaviour patterns embedded in all educational services are often difficult to 'see'. These two volumes present the reader with a clear picture of Soviet aims in preschool education and the means by which they are realized: the 'collective consciousness' ('mine is ours, ours is mine') which guides attitudes to property and the role of the individual as member of a group, and discourages 'individualistic' play; the involvement of the larger community in the work of each school so that members of the collective visit the school, get to know the children, make toys for them, take them on outings, and invite them to the place in which the collective members work; the relatively small influence of parents who, rather than being left to bring up their children unguided, are helped to bring up their children properly by the model of Socialist education which each kindergarten represents: these are some of the controversial ideas which could well prompt Western parents, teachers and administrators to take a close look at themselves and the values that have become habitual to them.

It is interesting to compare the differences in upbringing in two different social systems and the two different ideologies which support them. For this purpose we recommend:

URIE BRONFENBRENNER, *Two Worlds of Childhood: U.S.A. and U.S.S.R.*, Allen & Unwin, London, 1972; Penguin Education, Harmondsworth, 1974. (Published in U.S.A. as URIE BRONFENBRENNER and JOHN C. CONDRY, *Two Worlds of Childhood: U.S.A. and U.S.S.R.*, Russell Sage, New York, 1970.)

JILL and PENDARELL KENT, *Nursery Schools for All*, Ward Lock Educational, London, 1972; International Publications Service, New York, 1971.

This book deals with the reasons why all children should have the opportunity of nursery education, and with the day-to-day running of nursery classes. The authors speak eloquently of the way in which a school can be run and draw on their wide knowledge of this area of education as well as on the practical experience of running their own school.

KORNEI CHUKOVSKY (translated and edited by Miriam Morton), *From Two to Five*, University of California Press, London and Berkeley, 1966.

Chukovsky is a much loved author of Russian children's books, a scholar of adult literature and a student of children, of their speech, their learning patterns and their use of fantasy in adjusting to reality. Unfortunately, this is an abridged version of the original work *Little Children*. The chapter dealing with the way Russian children learn language is omitted almost entirely. We are left with delightful quotations such as: 'Once when we were taking a walk on the beach, Lialia saw, for the first time, a ship in the distance: "Mommie, Mommie, the locomotive is taking a bath!" she cried with excitement and amazement.' Throughout the book the author shows his delight in children and their use of language. His knowledge of language development and of children's linguistic creativity are set down with sympathy and eloquence.

E. M. MATTERSON, *Play With a Purpose For Under-Sevens*, Penguin, Harmondsworth, 1975.

For parents who wish to reach a greater understanding of the meaning of children's play, this is a practical and stimulating book, full of advice about the materials children need and the ways in which they can be helped to learn through their play.

D. W. WINNICOTT, *The Child, the Family and the Outside World*, Pelican, Harmondsworth and Baltimore, 1964; William Gannon, Santa Fé.

A child-psychiatrist presents the world of children to the general reader. Dr Winnicott deals with mother–child, parent–child and child–school relationships and in doing so discusses many topics which have become problem areas for parents. He writes about children's behaviour and parent's attitudes in a clear and sympathetic manner.

See also:

D. W. WINNICOTT, *Playing and Reality*, Tavistock Publications, London, 1971; Pelican, Harmondsworth, 1974; Basic Books, New York, 1971.

BEATRIX TUDOR-HART, *Toys, Play and Discipline in Childhood*, Routledge, London, 1970; Fernhill House, New York, 1971.

Books on Children Making and Doing

RUTH AINSWORTH (compiler), (illustrated by Bernadette Watts), *Look, Do and Listen*, Heinemann, London, 1969; Watts, New York, 1969.

A miscellany of stories, verses, games, recipes, gardening hints and instructions for making and doing some of the things that young children can find exciting.

ELIZABETH M. GREGG and BOSTON'S CHILDREN'S MEDICAL CENTRE STAFF (editors), *What To Do When There's Nothing To Do*, Hutchinson, London, 1969; Delacorte, New York, 1968.

Nearly 600 ideas for things to do based on ingenious ways of using very ordinary household objects to distract and delight children.

ELIZABETH GUNDREY (illustrated by Martin Mayhew), *Fun With Art*, Scroll Press, New York, 1973.

A book full of ideas for making pictures using familiar tools as well as unlikely ones like a sponge and a toothbrush. Equally unusual materials are also suggested. The instructions are presented in picture-strip form and are easy to understand. A book which will help older children and parents to enliven painting and picture-making at home.

FELICIA LAW (illustrated by Gunvor Edwards), *Something To Make*, Puffin, Harmondsworth and Baltimore, 1971.

Making things from odds and ends of household junk. A collection of practical suggestions made by an experienced teacher of art and handicraft.

HENRY PLUCKROSE (editor), *Starting Points Series*, Evans Brothers, London.

RITA DAVIES, *Let's Paint*, Evans Brothers, London, 1971.

ROGER TINGLE, *Let's Print*, Evans Brothers, London, 1971.

GUY SCOTT, *Let's Crayon*, Evans Brothers, London, 1971.

RITA DAVIES, *Let's Make a Picture*, Evans Brothers, London, 1971.

Starting Points, addressed to children, show how to use a number of different picture-making techniques. In each book, colour illustrations accompany a page of instructions.

SEPTIMA, *Something To Do*, Puffin, Harmondsworth, 1966. Suggestions for games to play, things to make and do for each month of the year.

3 The Beginning of Language

In the earliest months of babyhood, talk is not yet established as something the baby himself does. We listen for the baby's first words with special anticipation. We know he will begin to talk one day, without knowing when. What we are much less aware of (for the very good reason that it is not easy to see it happen) is the baby's ability to listen. We notice his reaction to noise, to sounds, to light, to colour. We understand much less what the baby does in reacting to the talk he hears directed to him.

Even in the most 'unfavoured' environments babies very soon after their birth show signs of reaction to language – as though they have a 'sense' for picking up from all the noise flying about in the air just these sounds from which they will begin to 'put the language together'. They respond willingly and eagerly to gentle, affectionate speech – the *only* speech which should be directed to a baby. Their *need* to listen in this way (for the child to feel secure, to feel he is 'being talked to', and to have a helpful model of 'noise' from which he can learn language) is often overlooked or plainly ignored. Often babies are talked to according to the fluctuating adult mood; sometimes in a good mood – as a little girl would talk to a doll – sometimes in a bad mood as one talks about a nuisance: 'You mess yourself again and . . .,' 'I haven't got the time to be with you all the time' and the like. This is perplexing and confusing to the infant child because it is impossible for him to make sense of the changes in attitude which are conveyed by such talk. Uncertainty and fear will then bedevil his learning.

Before a baby develops language he discovers, by means of his babbling, the complex sets of muscles of his speech organs – the lips, the tongue, the glottis, the vocal chords. Babbling, like scribbling in sound, is the baby's way of exercising these muscles and practising so as to be able to produce at will certain sounds. He passes from babbling to differentiated speech sounds much as he passes from squirming and random movements to crawling. But to do so he needs to have achieved four states of readiness.

First, his brain is developing to give him muscular control over the complex vocal apparatus. Second, he is listening to the sounds of the language used around him. Third, he is discovering how to link speech sounds to specific situations. Fourth, he is discovering how to understand something of what is said to him and to respond to it: he is learning that some of his speech sounds can be made so as to carry messages to which others will respond. In short, he is learning to function with sound in order to get things done for him, to ask for things, to accompany his desires, to point. He now abandons his babbling and begins to share in the language game.

One part of the infant's earliest participation in language is not only to name people and things but to get things done for him, to regulate the behaviour of other people, to express his feelings, to make friends. Learning *how to mean* is learning how to function deliberately in terms of oral interactions with other people in a variety of ways. The other part of his participation is of course concerned with the way his listening interacts with those who talk to him.

While a baby babbles, producing sounds like all other babies, we cannot tell how much he is learning from listening to us. We may find him producing a voice tune which he heard when he heard someone say: 'Up we go. Down we go.' Or when he is bathed, feeling the water move around him, he may sing the tune of 'Splash the water'. However, almost by instinct many adults speak as though they were bent on ensuring the child's understanding of what they say. At the same time they also speak normally to other people in the baby's presence – and even to the baby himself – before he starts trying his first words. Taken altogether these experiences provide a variety of ways in which the baby hears language being used, and when those nearest him speak consistently with gentle persuasive voices, all other confusing language 'noises' do not worry him. Out of the many occasions when he hears and sees those around him talk, the tunes, the rhythm, the quality of the voice, the expressions on the faces, the loudness or softness of voices, all begin to make special 'sense'. From this point of view he is no longer the universal baby. He is *becoming* an English baby, a Chinese, American or Nigerian baby. He is becoming a native 'listener' thus a native speaker: a Cockney, a Geordie, or Glaswegian.

To describe the baby as a speaker at this stage is of course a very special use of the term 'speaker'. He does not speak as we speak. He has a 'special language' of his own. This special language contains both features from the speech of people around him and his own characteristics from the way he comes to exploit his own voice. So some of his speech sounds are like those of the people around him, some are not. What he does with them will not be easily understood by outsiders. His family will readily interpret these and know his meanings because they are part of the situations out of which his meanings come. His 'special language' is the first stage in his becoming a 'speaker' in the adult sense, it is the road that leads from his 'no-language' to meaningful language. His gurgling is no longer the gurgling of all the world's babies for he is already receiving an intensive training of his phonological abilities. His sounds are beginning to follow a certain phonetic direction which will allow him to build his 'words'. And at the same time he begins to decode the sounds directed to him as messages that he can 'understand'.

Once the baby begins to 'talk' he needs to hear the language spoken to him without self-consciousness and without his talk being quoted back to him. For the child is trying to build up his model of language on the pattern of the language spoken around him. To give him 'baby' noises is to keep him unnecessarily at a stage that he not only needs to overcome but which he is trying to overcome. He needs to extend his control of the language steadily towards adult language and for this he needs the appropriate 'feed-back' which comes when adults offer the child a due share of their talk – as one of the family community.

In the short space of time during which the child's language has begun to grow he will already have established within himself a model of how the world seems to him and of how he sees himself inside this world, according to the information which his environment gives him. Both these models will be in a constant and rapid state of movement and change, especially in the first two years: from a sucking, squirming creature, blinded by strong light, whose world is filled with milk and sleep, the baby becomes an active, moving, gasping, sometimes noisy creature with an established personal identity, ready for inter-action.

Learning language is not just a question of making sounds, or words, or sentences. It is also a question of learning what language will do, of how language can be used. Among the first spoken utterances the child establishes are several like those shown in Nigel's 'portrait' (pp. 38–43). Like Nigel, all children 'invent' words which may be very unlike those they hear around them. As soon as child and adult establish between them the meanings of these 'words', that is, as soon as the adults pick up the clues the child gives about how he is using his words, they have established a language link. The child has requirements. He 'invents' the words with which to communicate these. He repeats these. Adults grasp his meanings and everything is under way for the child to become a language user.

He is no sooner embarked on the naming game than he begins to invent sentences. He hears sentences like 'I'll get the ball for you.' He speaks sentences like 'Jom a baw-baw.' Again the adults learn the meanings of these 'invented' sentences as they did with the child's earlier invented words which he eventually discards. They are able to construct the adult equivalents of 'Jom a baw-baw' according to the situation: '(I) John want the ball,' '(I) John am going to throw the ball on the floor,' '(I) John don't want the ball any more.'

The child's speech from the very beginning establishes the purpose of spoken language – to link meanings to sounds and to grasp meanings from sounds. This is a task of great complexity about which not too much is known yet. We notice that at a particular stage children will say 'I goed up stairs,' 'Mummy buyed a present for you,' and, as Nigel did, speak a positive and add the negative by shaking his head: 'goat shouldn't eat lid . . . [*shaking his head*] good for it'. Stephen, with a much more developed grammar, produced the sentences: 'Then he will go under that bridge now and the diesel train is going under that bridge too. Do you like this bridges? Bridges are cobway in't it? And in't they? . . .'

The child does not need constant reminders of what he does differently from adults in his sentences for he will learn from us more than we can teach him. This is possible only because his capacity to learn is so great. In making sentences children's main purposes are to express feelings and needs, to communicate facts, to inquire and speculate. At the same time they are trying out their language and testing it against the responses they receive from people who know it. The child is also learning from those around him something of the quality of their affection, their attitudes to life, their kinds of behaviour. From this he is going to build up the semantic structure which will support his language – the child can only discover the meanings of the words he uses from the linguistic environment in which he lives. Learning to speak like the people around him is his most significant step to becoming a native *within* a specific environment, a specific culture.

By the age of three many children have acquired a remarkable vocabulary and a complex grammar. They have also had time and experience to realize that language will do things for them.

Functions of Language: Some Examples

As learners of language, it is not just language that we are learning, not just words and sentences that we learn to speak and understand. At the same time we learn how to use language for special purposes: to submit to the power of those around us; to rebel; to learn who we are; to speak with ourselves; to learn on our own and in co-operation or in competition with others.

The following examples of children learning what language will do for them illustrate a small part of the range of uses to which we put our language in our quest for meaning in the search for reality. Without help from adults who listen carefully and offer many examples of how language can be used, learning of this kind does not take place. For children can learn only from what they are exposed to.

This account of functions of language – what language will do for the young child – draws upon the work of Professor M. A. K. Halliday and Dr Joan Tough:*

It will get things done. The right 'sentence' will bring some milk or get some one to pick up something that has dropped.

It will stop things happening. 'Don't do that.' 'Don't touch the fruit in the bowl.'

It will allow one to claim things for oneself. 'That my train.' 'Give me that. It mine.' 'You can't have that it's mine.'

It will help form friendships and gain cooperation. 'You look at my book with me.' 'You be a lion.' 'You can have some egg.' 'You play with me.' 'You get birdie for me.' 'Draw train for me.'

*See Books for Further Reading (pp. 229–30).

It will help to change the form of an activity. 'Now birdie flies away. Now we go to find birdie. Where birdie? In tree. We go up up. Climb up to see birdie. We can make a house in the tree and birdie can come and see us.'

It will convey information, report or discover information. 'Well, this is an old old train they used to have before diesels. It went from London to Edinburgh.' 'Where Edinburgh?' 'A long way away in Scotland.' 'Where Scotland?' 'I know how tika go, I show.'

It will enable questions to be asked: How? Why? Where? When? What? Who? Discovering the environment is based on such question starters. 'Why dog bark?' 'How ticka make tic tic?' 'Why lemon make faces?' 'Why this triangle?' 'Why paper tear?'

It will enable doubts and disagreements to be expressed and propositions and speculations to be made. 'This a dog.' 'This a woolly dog.' 'No, it is a lamb.' 'Lamb not dog? Not woolly dog?' 'NO, woolly lamb.' 'Why birdie has feathers? Why dog not has feathers? Why mans not have feathers?'

'I think it is a pond. It's a fountain. Look there's some bubbly water. It's not working properly. It should have a big long water coming up. It's tired now and it's just going bubbly bubbly a little. Then it'll go woosh and be a big long water fountain.'

'No, I think they've turned the water down.' 'Why?' 'Probably because there's too much wind and it blows the water about and makes people wet.' 'Why does the wind blow the water?' . . .

It will be used to describe incidents and tell stories. 'Birdie has two eyes . . . one eye there, one eye there. Birdie can see you. Birdie can have a rest here to sleep in and he can look at you and then fly ooops on your head.'

It will be used to guess at what may happen. 'Why is the lion in a cage?' 'What do you think?' 'Because he was captured and doesn't want to be in a cage.' 'What do you think would happen if there was no cage for him?' 'I would run away if I was lion.' 'What else?' 'I would run far away.' 'Suppose he ran away to our garden.' 'I would give him some food and we could make a house for him.' 'What if he wanted to eat you up?' 'Oh . . .' 'Perhaps he would if he was very hungry.' 'Nooo, he wouldn't. He would have a lot of food . . . and I could leave it for him to eat . . . and then we could take him to Africa . . .'

4 Children and Parents: Five Portraits

We had two main choices concerning the form of this section: the first possibility was to keep talking about 'the child' and his development in a theoretical and abstract manner and hence about an equally abstract and theoretical child, adding a few concrete examples to 'illustrate' the theory. The second possibility – the one we chose – was to select, from the limited amount of information we have, a few 'portraits' of real children and let them speak for themselves. This would then allow us to refer to theory only to add a few 'touches' to the 'living theory' which these real children illustrate. The examples we have chosen show the way in which the child's language develops and – more important – the way it *should* be encouraged to develop by those around the child.

In the first portrait we follow Nigel for a few months from the time he speaks his first words to his creation of sentences. The second, Stephen, shows how much the use of language enters into the activities of a child under three. The third is a remarkable statement of a mother's concern for her children when she was confronted with establishing a home in a new flat in a tower block; the fourth is a group portrait of children speaking and writing about life as they understand it, and the fifth is an imaginative story written by Patrick at home, bridging his last days as a preschool child and his first experiences of school.

In all except the third, the parents are very much in the background; it is the child who speaks. It must be said that some of the children – Nigel, Stephen and Patrick – are in optimal conditions. Nigel's parents are professionally interested in language, his father being a professor of linguistics and his mother a doctor of philosophy and a lecturer. They are very aware of the amount of time they should spend talking and playing with Nigel and following his development. They take great care choosing what is right for him – toys, stories, rhymes, story books – and Nigel's language developed quickly and confidently. Patrick's situation is similar – father an architect, mother a specialist in French language studies. They too give much attention to everything concerning Patrick's development. We are well aware that these parents are sociologically 'non-average' people. In choosing these models we do not try to prove anything about average language development but simply the importance that *interaction with the environment* has in the child's language development, and the *quality* of the attention parents must give to the child's needs. A lot of non-middle-class children get attention of similar quality, but their 'portraits' are much harder to find. We are lucky to have the portrait of Mrs Chrissy Channel. The fourth 'portrait' shows a variety of four and five year olds from a variety of backgrounds, by no means exclusively middle-class.

Nigel

We begin with fragments of baby talk taken at short intervals between his tenth and twentieth months.

Nigel at ten and a half months has a complex communication system, although it might well be thought too simple to bother about. Because we are concerned so much with what language will do for us, with what we mean and not with what language is or how we transmit our meanings to other people, we tend to be unaware how complicated language learning is. But when set down with the insight of the linguist, however, it is possible to catch a glimpse of what goes on all the time language is being used:

(1) *Nigel needs to get things done for him.*

Nigel has learned that we use language to make things happen. Language is an instrument for making others act for him. His speech

tunes fall as they would were we to say 'thank you': THANK YOU

He says 'na na na na' and means 'give me that.' When he uses 'na' his demand is urgent. When he wants his little bird with the whirring tail, he makes a sound like the first part of the French word *boeuf* – boeu.

(2) *Nigel learns to use language to regulate the behaviour of other people.*

He says 'genng' and means 'do that again'. But when he wants something done right away he says 'mnng' loudly, meaning 'do that right now'.

(3) *Nigel learns to use language to convey his own feelings with no reference to other people.*

He has two ways of using language for this purpose: one to withdraw from the scene and one to participate. He makes a 'yawning' word which means 'I'm sleepy.'

When he is pleased with something generally he says 'a', meaning 'that's nice' or when eating, 'nng' meaning 'that tastes nice.'

When he is interested in something he says 'e' which means 'look! That's interesting.' And when he is drawn to something that interests him, he says 'daw' meaning 'a dog' or 'boeu' meaning 'birds.'

(4) *Nigel learns to use language to show friendliness and to respond to other people.*

In interacting with other people Nigel has already learned to start a conversation. He makes friendly noises to claim a person for himself and to involve this person in what he is doing. He says 'e da da' meaning 'nice to see you, and shall we look at this together?'

But if kept waiting he uses quite a different tack 'annn nnna' meaning 'nice to see you . . . at last.' And when conversation and activity has been initiated he responds with 'e' and 'a' (the last as in drink*a* pint*a* milk*a*) meaning 'yes?' and 'I see.'

The stage from which these few fragments have been taken is followed by one important discovery: that language can be used to recall the past, to talk about experiences after they have happened and to refer to things that are not present.

At 18 months Nigel has begun to master this use of language.

[*Nigel picks up a plastic egg*].

NIGEL: 'a-y-i.' [egg . . . egg, *meaning 'my egg'*] 'o' [*surprise, at finding another egg inside it*] 'a-y-i . . . a-y-i . . . a-y-i . . .' [egg . . . egg . . . egg . . ., *repeated as he continues to discover one egg inside another*] 'ndou mbaw' [no more, *when he reaches the smallest egg and the last one*].

Later the same day:

MOTHER: 'Did you tell Daddy what you had for tea?'

NIGEL: 'a-y-i . . . o . . . a-y-i' [egg . . . ooh egg, *repeated excitedly*]. 'gawgl gaw gwa' [cockadoodledoo, *meaning 'cockerel', but also 'cock' on the cornflakes packet and hence 'cornflakes'. This he extends to 'weathercock' so, as he has just been out for walk past the church, he continues his inventory of things seen.*] 'tika' [sticks].

MOTHER: 'You don't have sticks for tea.'

NIGEL: 'law-oo' [and holes].

MOTHER: 'You didn't have sticks and holes for tea!'

NIGEL: [*returning to the subject of tea*] 'douba' [and toast].

At twenty months Nigel communicates more extensively. His language is beginning to sound like our language – although it is still an intimate one which outsiders will not readily understand. The conventions he uses are shared by him and a few people around him. They understand very clearly what he means. On paper it is possible to convey only a small part of the total speech act he creates: his voice quality, his speech tunes, his gestures must be imagined.

1 July

NIGEL: 'd a oo . . . tebl . . . jooga . . . poon' [down . . . table . . . sugar . . . spoon . . ., *meaning 'put the sugar down on the table so that I can dip my spoon in'*]. 'aw-ooba vaw ja' [open for you, *meaning 'open it for me'*].

Nigel will continue to say 'you' meaning 'me' for some time.

Ten days later: 11 July

NIGEL: 'make cross tickmatic . . . in Dada room . . .' ['let's make a cross on the typewriter in Daddy's room']

17 July

Nigel is at home after a visit to the zoo. He is remembering something that happened and the discussion that took place at the time. What happened and the discussion of what happened together form the event:

NIGEL: 'try eat lid.'

DADDY: 'what tried to eat the lid?'
NIGEL: 'try eat lid.'
DADDY: 'what tried to eat the lid?'
NIGEL: 'goat . . . man said no . . . goat try eat lid . . . man said no.'
Later returning to the same theme:
NIGEL: 'goat try eat lid . . . man said no . . . goat shouldn't eat lid . . . good for it' [*accompanied by a shake of the head as an expression of the negative, thus meaning 'not good for it'*]. 'goat try eat lid . . . man said no . . . goat shouldn't eat lid . . . good for it . . .'

21 September

Nigel is looking at a home-made scrap book on his own:
NIGEL: 'that a steam train . . . they taken it away . . . that a mountain train . . . it go . . . That train can't go any more . . . it old chuffa . . . it old old old old chuffa . . .' [*looking at a toy crane*] 'there no driver . . . how can crane go?'

In the morning Nigel is being dressed.

NIGEL: [*while being dressed*] 'it teatime.'
DADDY: 'No, it's breakfast time.'
NIGEL: 'it brekka time . . . want your milk . . . [I want my milk]

22 September (Aged twenty-four months)

Nigel is drawing.
NIGEL: 'have daddy pen . . . you be careful . . . don't get ink.'
DADDY: 'No don't get ink on your fingers.'
NIGEL: 'that where the chuffa go [*drawing a line*] shall we draw the chuffa on the railway line? shall we draw the chuffa on the railway line? train not going very well, train not going very well . . . that a green chuffa.'

The business of family life goes on around Nigel and he is part of it. His crawling and early walking are done among the family; his play is in among other people; his toys are among them. The room where he sleeps is open to the lights and sounds from beyond so that always he feels part of it all. He is happy to be on his own, to be engrossed in his own concerns from time to time because he is certain that when he needs someone – if only to say 'hallo' to, someone will be there, welcoming and ready to respond even if it is only to say: 'Go on, tell me about it, but notice I'm busy cooking.' He is one of the family but not *the* one of the family. He has rights but not more than others. He knows in what way those around him are important to one another. He learns from them how they show affection and extend their attention to one another and he becomes able to show concern and purpose as they do.

In two years, starting as though he were a stranger from outer space, this human baby has reached a point in learning the 'home' language at which he may very rightly claim to be an English speaker. To reach this point so quickly he has devoted a great part of his time and energy to listening and speaking. He has the good fortune to have a wholly sympathetic home in which to learn. He has a generous share of adult talk and adult attention. He talks both to himself and his toys as well as to other people; he listens to the talk of those around him and draws closer and closer to the language they use and to the ways in which they use it. By the time he is ready for school he will be likely to have at his command an impressive ability to use language for many purposes.

It is important to notice that in these fragments of dialogue no 'baby-talk' is directed to Nigel. His 'private' language is well understood and he appears to understand much of what is said to him. He is learning from the language he hears around him exactly what he needs. Like all of us he listens to the meaning of what he hears and not so much to its form. Like all of us he is identifying himself with the language of his parents (and later, with the language used by children at school).

It is also important to notice that Nigel like all children is corrected when he gets his facts wrong, not for having mistakes in the form of the language which expresses the facts. Thus on 21 September the following dialogue takes place:

NIGEL: 'It tea time.'
DADDY: 'No, it's breakfast time.'
NIGEL: 'It brekka time.'

In his father's response there is no reference to Nigel's use of 'it' as opposed to 'it's'. 'It's' may be in his listening; it will appear in his speaking when he is ready. By comparison, the confusion of tea-time with breakfast-time is considered important. It is immediately corrected and the correction is accepted and acknowledged by Nigel.

It is clear from studies of children entering school that the parents of a minority of children deliberately encourage baby-talk by using it themselves in talking to their child. The persistence of such talk is a measure of the alarming parental desire to preserve the 'baby' in their child, to restrict his growth in much more than language. Such children are almost always somewhat immature in all aspects of their behaviour of which their language immaturity is only one sign.

Stephen

Stephen is two years ten months old. His mother brings sympathy and warmth to the upbringing of her child without effusiveness and fuss. Her responses are gentle and natural. In the following extract, she used a tape recorder to catch Stephen's talk. Later, she wrote down as accurately as possible what she heard on the tape.

Stephen is playing with his trains when he should have been having his afternoon sleep.

STEPHEN: '... stepped over the train. Then he will go under that bridge now and the diesel train is going under that bridge too. Do you like this bridges? Bridges are cobway in't it? And when in't they? I know – cobway go ... go ... that's cobway falling down? Is it? Yes it is – you see – and when the train is covered in cobway the man said it's so stiff isn't he ?– The trains are covered with cobway when the man says, "Oh, I'm so stiff!".'

MOTHER: "Oh, you mean cobwebs ..."

STEPHEN: 'And why didn't he? You can read that book for a minute.'

MOTHER: 'Can I ... Thank you.'

STEPHEN: 'Yes while I play with my trains. That's the signal and the signal box is under the radiogram. And when ... at the moment really ... It's get ... diesel train.

'Must have one on the diesel train mustn't we? That will drive it off anyway. That man will drive it – you see? And why don't they lie down for? He's got a stick and why hasn't he got a stick for?'

MOTHER: 'To bonk people with.'

STEPHEN: 'Why? . . . Oh people get upset. And he – he – don't bonk – I take the stick away from him and . . . bonk me.'

MOTHER: 'Will you. ?'

STEPHEN: 'Yes, I'll put him in the water.'

MOTHER: 'What will you do to him then?'

STEPHEN: 'I'll put him down at the bottom and . . . k-k . . . pop up! Wouldn't that be interesting? . . .'

[*Stephen is in bed. It is about 7.30 a.m.*]

MOTHER: 'Be very careful now.'

STEPHEN: 'Oo – oo . . . what is this? It's a coat hanger . . .'

MOTHER: 'What do you want a coat hanger in bed for?'

STEPHEN: 'It's my ship really . . . It's sailing now. It's fallen into the water. It's lying in the water floating. It's all falling down. It's going to drop down and break itself – pggg!!!

'There! It's hanging on you.'

MOTHER: 'Coming for breakfast, Stephen?'

Here the tape recorder has caught Stephen's talk with the accuracy few of us have for remembering speech events. We are so much bound up with finding out what people mean – or what we think they mean – that we have only a rather vague notion of what is actually said. Stephen is not talking to another person. He is talking with himself and with what makes up his play. Occasionally he throws out a suggestion or a question to his mother: 'You can read that book for a minute . . . He's got a stick and why hasn't he got a stick for?' Otherwise his talk is an intricate part of his play and as we cannot see what he is doing, the man and the stick, for instance, are a little puzzling. (And were there cobwebs under the radiogram?)

However, the real trains are not far away in Stephen's mind – and real bridges too. He is playing with his trains and coming to terms with life as well. His thoughts tumble into sentences he begins and has not time to finish. So he begins another and in his playing makes sense of everything which he does not produce as speech.

Mrs Chrissy Channel

At times the events in a family's life are disturbed by changes affecting both children and parents. To move from the small-scale surroundings of streets of houses, markets and shops, with many relatives close to hand, to the impersonal surroundings of a tower block of flats, is the cause of much concern to mothers of young children. And where this brings with it separation from grandparents, relatives and friends, it is a change not without misgivings, the more so because, for those involved, there is no alternative. The price of a 'modern' home may all too often be paid in loneliness and alienation. Unless she is resourceful, the children will share this with their mother. Unless she is secure in her own life, she may find the task of helping her children to adjust happily to their new home beyond her.

To give comfort and security to others demands considerable inner strength and affection. The strain these new adjustments may cause is enough to produce fears and uncertainty in young women who in other surroundings are able to manage well enough. Retreat into long silences, because there is no one to talk to 'except the baby', will quickly affect the child. His welfare depends more on talking, on experimenting and discovering, and on having lively parents and friends around than on having modern, convenient kitchens and central heating (not that the two sets of provision are irreconcilable).

The conflicts produced by this problem are powerfully conveyed by a young mother who moved from a two-roomed flat in East London to a new tower block some way off, in the Isle of Dogs. In an interview she gave to BBC Radio London, she describes with affection the old and by no means perfect surroundings she grew up in, and in which she had her first two children:

I used to live in Hoxton. It was quite near the market, you know. It's where I was born so that I knew everybody there, and I'd walk down the market and never feel lonely. Right old buildings, you know – hundred year old – just two rooms in there. I lived on the second floor. Mostly old people lived there, been there since the war. I'd the two children while I was there. My eldest boy was two – it was only a small room – very very tiny but I used to get on all right there, you know. I think it was because I knew if I did get fed up I could go for a walk down the market or my mum lived round the corner or my nan – I was right near my nan. I'd always got someone to go round if I felt sort of under the weather. I was having my third baby. I'd had my second one I was having my third one so I just took the first thing that come along.

And the first thing that came along was a new flat in a Tower Block.

Mrs Channel recalls her own reactions to their move very clearly. She has great understanding of her children's problems – of their dismay and their disorientation at being transplanted into a concrete world. Her handling of the situation is remarkable for the way in which her patience and her knowledge of children's needs eased the situation for them. She readily takes the burden upon herself without complaint and sets about compensating for the loss of friends and relatives:

It was awful because there were only about three people in the block. It was awkward not knowing anyone to talk to – and I wasn't the sort of person who could go up and talk to someone and make conversation. I think once you've got children – like the welfare woman come round and I went round the welfare and you mix in with people, it's having the children you know – when you're walking along, people come up to you and talk to you just through having children – even at the shops. It's only small conversations but it means a lot when you're over here on your own all day long. It wasn't so bad for me as it was for the children – not getting them out, not knowing what to do with them all day long, keeping them occupied, stopping them getting frustrated because of not being able to get out enough. Daren was only a baby but Gary he was a bit of a problem. Being two, he took it badly. He went back to messing himself, you know. Well, I spent more time with him so that he didn't feel lonely. I'd give him things to do. If I could I took him out for walks and showed him what the new surroundings were like so that he'd see they weren't all that frightening. Tried to bring him to terms with it, you know, trying to bring him round to show him what it was like. And he understood, because sometimes when I went back to where we used to live he'd say: 'Well that was our old house.' And he knew that this was his new house. Well when we come to view the place, we brought him with us and so I let him walk through the flat and he told me exactly what bedroom he wanted. I wanted him to get used to it right from the beginning to know he had to have a change. I think a lot of it was to do with having the new baby. But I was lucky really because a young girl moved in on the third floor down from me and she used to bring her little boy up and they'd play together. I'd give them things to play with. It passed the time more for him as well. The girl and I did become close friends that way.

This is only part of Mrs Channel's portrait; a further part dealing with the provisions she makes for her children's play is to be found in Chapter 2, pages 20–21.

Five-Year Olds as Talkers and Writers

In the portraits which follow we see glimpses of the expanding world of childhood and some of the ways in which two groups of children come to terms with experience. They give an image of themselves very different from the way many adults writers have envisaged children.

THE TALKERS

(From an Inner-City Nursery School)

The first set of texts came from a nursery class in an inner-city school. Here the children paint pictures on large sheets of coloured paper. Their teacher takes great interest in what they are doing. When he has finished a picture each child takes it to her and talks freely about it. She records exactly what each child wants written on the picture and later other interested children listen while the painters talk about what they have done. The paintings then go up on the walls of the classroom and the corridor. Children are pleased to see their work displayed in this way and often want to hear the stories on the pictures read by the teacher.

Andy (4 years): A picture about firemen.

Four poles with two men climbing down, they've coming to America they are sliding up and down because they have a tummy ache, they eat poison things. Too many sweets.

Harry (4 years): A man dancing.

He has two eyes so he can see, a nose that's why he can breathe, one mouth so he can talk to the animals.

A fire.

A lady she's right down there she can't get out and the lady said I can't look at the fire it makes my eyes blind.

Ian (4 years 6 months): A house with a great burning sun.

That's the sun shining and all that different stuff come out the sun, there's a house and its got a chimney for smoke to come out of. The wind is blowing all washing.

Jimmy (4 years 8 months): A house with a large figure and a small figure.

The house is for me and for somebody in the house. Daddy's in the house. A doggy shouts and he wake me up. I was sleeping and he pushed me out in the garden, right out in the garden and locked me out. I pushed the door and I come in again. I go to sleep again.

Rose (4 years 9 months): A house, a man, fishes, water and moon.

A fish catching a fisherman then the boat go up in the hills and the fisherman fell under the fish water. The fish bite him and he got away. There's the moon up, the houses and balloons round it, flying up in the sky and pulling the house up as well.

Tom (4 years 8 months): A house with figures.

A house with a woman living in it, and she have a man who fights and she get the gun and she shoot and he's a dead man.

The subject matter is unexpected and its expression idiosyncratic, fantastic and at times poetic: far away from the stereotypes often presented as 'child's language'. These children make use of very different narrative patterns, for the contexts from which their narratives arose are different.

In the case of the inner-city children the context is created not only by means of language, as in the case of all story-telling, but by other means as well, in this case pictures. In these samples, language is used to clarify certain aspects of the action which 'happen' *in the picture*. Thus their samples only make sense when they are taken together with the pictures of which they are part.

Each picture – what *we* see simply as a picture – represents a whole discourse inside the child's head of which only a part – certain functional sentences – are given linguistic form. These sentences make aspects of their inner discourse available to others.

The fantastic and sometimes poetic feeling which these 'picture-texts' produce in us is partly explained by the fact that the reader must attempt to reconstruct *the whole structure of meanings* without the essential visual information.

In contrast, the narratives of the suburban children which now follow are not dependent on complementary pictures. The semantic structure (the structure of meanings) flows directly out of the linguistic structure. There is no ambiguity: they are able to make available what they want to tell the reader. Their treatment of time, action and causality is clear and explicit; there are elements of scientific thinking ('two clouds they bang together and the rain drops') and social ideologies ('Do you know how the rain stops? God is up in heaven...' – or Mandy's review of the elements of the bourgeois way of life – babies+house+garden+holiday+money ... and Daddy working hard to get everything) formalized in their narratives. They used more 'public' elements in the construction of their samples, for their speech is addressed to an audience, as opposed to the self-addressed, reflexive sentences of the inner-city children.

In addition, different ways of talking are used by each group of children, for each comes from a different environment with its own linguistic patterns. A careful description of dialect features and the different linguistic practices in the upbringing of children in both environments – the abundance or lack of interaction with adults and peer groups, of story telling, story reading, picture book discussions, etc. – will make much clearer these differences in linguistic development.

From a Suburban Nursery School

In this second set of texts, from a suburban nursery school, the news sessions are filled with voluble, sometimes urgent communications to which other children listen with interest. Audience participation is another important aspect of the 'public' language these children have learned to produce. It is at once obvious that these children are at home with their language and with themselves.

Jonathan (4 years 10 months):

Sometimes when there is a thunderstorm, it makes a pattern like a zig-zag and when it rains, inside the clouds is a big bowl and when there are two clouds they bang together and the rain drops down on the trees and sometimes it drips off the trees and looks as if it is still raining.

Once when I was getting my dinner the rain started to pour down and once when I was in bed I heard the thunder. I thought someone was coming in the door but when I got out of bed nobody was there – I was all in the dark and could not go to sleep. I kept thinking it was morning but it was still night, and my sister was asleep so I put my fingers in my ears so that I could not hear the thunder. When it stopped thundering I got up and I was glad it was morning.

Do you know how the rain stops? God is up in heaven and when he moves his hands the sun shines very bright and the ground dries and the rain goes half way up and then right up into the big bowl.

Mandy (5 years):

Well, once upon a time there was a little girl called Kathryn and she very much wanted a baby, so one day her mother quickly went to hospital and the next day she come back with a sweet little baby and they called her Kathy and she grew up to be a beautiful girl with golden curls.

So Kathryn and Kathy grew very well together and one day Kathy so much wanted a house with a little corner garden. Mummy said they could get a house, but could not go for a holiday as well, because a house would cost too much money but Daddy worked and worked such a lot that they had enough money to go for a holiday. So Daddy said they would go to Spain.

The next day they packed their suitcases very very early and drove to the Airport. So the passengers took the car and pushed it into a very dark part of the aeroplane and the lady went round saying: 'All ladies and gentlemen and children, fasten your belts,' because do you know what, when you start off it is a bit bumpy and suddenly it goes very fast like a crash, because they are trying to get the plane off the ground. Then there was a great roar of running. They went so fast that they landed up in the air. This is how aeroplanes fly.

Before Kathy could believe her eyes, she saw two little villages below because the sky is so high and all you see is like blue, but it is really as big as the whole world. It just goes on and on and on and it looks as if the houses are as high as the sky, but they are not really, and there is an Eiffel Tower which you can see when you fly over Paris and it looks like Jack and the Beanstalk and that is the end.

Jane (5 years):

Once upon a time there was a little girl and she lived far off on a great big hill. It was very tall and high, and her house was right on the top of it. She could see far. She could see Big Ben and other big buildings and towers, but she could not see the bus. She was much too far up. She could just see a red spot going along, and one day, when her Mummy wasn't looking she did a very naughty thing. She went down the hill and got on the bus and went to see her Nanny. She thought that was very clever, but it was not; it was very naughty.

'Where have you been without Mummy and Daddy?' Nanny said, 'I came to see you.' But Nanny was not at all pleased. But *she* thought she was very clever to get on a bus on her own.

Her Mummy and Daddy were searching and searching all over the town and they never thought of Nanny's house. When they arrived home they said suddenly, 'Yes, I have got it, Nanny's house.'

So they went to see, but the little girl was home by then and she made herself a cup of tea on her own, and burned her fingers.

Then Mummy and Daddy came home. 'Where have you been?' They were cross, and put her straight to bed. 'I went to Nanny's, then I came home.' And they said 'Nanny's. You must not get on a bus on your own.' 'I did, I did,' she said. 'I got on a bus.'

Catherine (5 years):

I was thinking about when I grow up I would like to be a skater and what lessons I would have and what I would do. It would be so lovely to be a skater and I want to be a ballet dancer, two things I want to be because once I watched it on television and that gives me the idea.

I want to be a champion, and I asked my Mummy if I would get money, but Mummy said, 'No, you do it for the fun of doing it,' and I am going to do it for the fun of it and I am going to be a ballet dancer. I wonder what I will do. I expect I will be on my toes most of the time. I hope it doesn't make my toes ache.

That is the end of what I was thinking.

THE WRITERS

William (5 years 6 months):

On the ninth of June it was my dad's birthday. We bought him two cards and a pen and a thermometer. He was very satisfied. My dad said 'Thank you.' There were 4 things. The thermometer was yellow and it showed maximum and minimum. Maximum was the highest and minimum was the shortest.

David (5 years 9 months):

Once upon a time there lived an old scarecrow.

He frightened the birds away in fright but he wanted the birds to come and nest in him so he said 'Please come and nest in me little birds.'

'No,' said the birds.

'Please, please come and nest.'

'No,' said the birds. 'We have to fly to a hotter country to live.'

'Do you like it?'

'No, no' said the birds.

'I have some straw.'

'We don't care.'

So he just went to sleep and he was happy. The little birds were happy. He never saw the little birds again. At lunch he thought about the little birds.

Robert (5 years 8 months):

On Sunday I tidied the house up and my Mummy was very happy and she liked the floor. I was going out to play on my bike.

When I got up from bed we could not find the towel and in the night I dreamed about a dragon. I dreamed about mummy as well.

I am going to a party. Andrew will go to the swimming bath with someone I know. He is called Philip. I have not done the invitation. 'Yes' said my Daddy to me, 'you have not done the invitation.' I am going to do it when I get home.

Yesterday I got some new shoes and I had to go on the bus and I have got my new shoes on today and in the bus I was hot and in the night I was wanting my new shoes on. I waited for a long time and then I said to my Mummy, 'Can me and Andrew get dressed?'

All these accounts show children trying to understand the world about them. Sometimes this is an ordinary world of rather humdrum activities; at other times it is a strange haunting world as in David's story of the scarecrow. Sometimes there is a remarkable understanding of all sides of a situation, as in Jane's story of her visit to her Nanny: while one understands her parents' concern about the way a small child took herself off on a bus ride, one cannot but marvel at the triumph in her voice when she says: 'I did. I did. I got on a bus.' Perhaps the fact that the story is told in the third person allows her to describe her parents' plight and her own bold adventuring with such commendable fairness and without losing the genuine flash of rebellion. Mandy, on the other hand, shows how convenient the world is that she lives in. All her desires, for a baby, for a new house, for a holiday, are granted without difficulty. Her description of how aeroplanes fly is surely one of the most delightful to be found anywhere. Catherine's 'thinking' about growing up, although it is very typical of many little girls, has a touch of resignation in it as she contemplates the aching toes of the ballet dancer she longs to become. 'I expect I will be on my toes most of the time' might well be applied to all children as they grapple with the serious business of living, of coming to terms with themselves and the world. In this they reflect the influences of those around them and the quality of the life they share. Already all of them have put a prodigious amount of learning between them and babyhood.

A Story Called *Roy the Boy*

Patrick began to write this story in a small note-book at home while he was attending a nursery school. The version which follows has been altered to comply with conventional spelling, punctuation and the use of upper- and lower-case letters. The figures in square brackets indicate the page numbers in Patrick's manuscript.*

Roy the Boy

[1] Once there was a man. He was terribly brave. When he was going to fly he would always carry a parachute with him. One day he went to the aeroplane place and he [2] bought a do-it-yourself aeroplane and when he finished it his wife Marbella would go to the licence shop and get a licence. After all of that [3] the man let his wife test it to see if it was broken, which it was not, and after the test they had a lovely time flying in the air. [4] And on the 13th of May Marbella and his father had a baby named Roy. Roy was a very good baby. As soon as he got home [5] he went to sleep, he was so tired. And he did not have a cot to sleep in. When Roy's Mother and Father realized this they went to the cot shop and bought a cot. When they got home [6] they put the sweet baby in his cot. In the morning it was Roy's birthday. There were cakes and jelly and jam tarts. Roy was so pleased he jumped up and down and went dum de dum de all the time. [7] He got presents and badges and birthday cards. The next day he got more presents and especially a lovely pillow sheet to put on his pillow. That night Roy dreamed of presents and pillow sheets. [8] In the morning he saw his badges and realized

*Some pages of Patrick's original manuscript and an exact transcript of the text are shown from page 216 onwards.

that he was two years old. He was really pleased . . . danced up and down. The second time he jumped up he jumped right out of his cot. [9] After that it was breakfast. Roy ate his before Marbella and her father. On Tuesday it was Roy's birthday again and it was just the same thing. [10] One day Roy was having a lovely time flying in the air with his mum and dad. The brave man's name was Superstrong. One day their house caught fire! [11] And nobody knew! But Superstrong did. He got his ladder and rescued Roy. But Roy's mother escaped herself and met Superstrong and [12] Roy in the garden getting water to put out the fire. Then in five minutes the fire was out. Then after, they went to the [13] plane and got the map of England and went all over London to find a place to live in but they could not. Luckily they had two camp beds and two sleeping bags with them and the cot. [14] In the morning they were setting off again but this time just as they were taking off, a man shouted. 'Don't go. You can live with me.' So they stopped and asked if they had a [15] place to put their aeroplane. 'Yes', said the man, 'there is enough room in my garage for one million ants to live in.' Just then they had another test but it would not go so the [16] man went back to his home and got some rope and his car. When he got back he tied one end of the rope to the aeroplane and [the] other to his car and he towed the plane to his garage. [17] After that the man backed his car into the garage as well because the plane was mended of course. In the morning they were very pleased to be saved, [18] so they thanked the man. After all this they set off again. They were still very pleased of being [saved] as anyway their car [19] was blown up in the fire. On the 18th of May last they found a place to live in. They looked all around the unidentified house. [20] After the expedition they unpacked the map and the camp beds and the sleeping bags and the cot. After, they went to the police to see if they knew the fire and if they could live in the [21] house. Meanwhile in the middle of the night Roy woke up. Then he heard a sound. It went like this: 'Woo hoo.' Roy thought it was a ghost. He trembled for a moment. Then he remembered [22] he was three years old. So big boys of that age could not be scared of a ghost. So he went back to bed and had a good long sleep. For he missed breakfast. His mother Marbella had to kiss [23] him 20 times to wake him up. In the morning Roy had to go to school. For the first time he went Marbella had to come with him. He had to learn prayers [24] and especially work to do. Roy got home. He went to his bed to have a sleep. He found a toy gun. It was called Marx M-16. Roy had a [25] great time playing with his toy gun. Then he got bored and wanted something else to do. He went out in the garden and look who he saw: Marbella and [26] Superstrong flying about in the aircraft they had bought. Superstrong jumped off and picked up Roy and flew up again. It was much better than shooting nothing! Indeed [27] it was not. Roy told Marbella to stop the aircraft a minute so that he could get his gun to play with in the plane. [28] [Illustration with speech balloon 'Don't worry, we're landing, Roy'] [29] Roy said 'When is it my birthday again?' 'February', said Superstrong. 'It's January now, Roy.' Years passed but Roy was sad. He had [30] no friend at school. He was seven by the time he had a friend. Before he had a friend his mother was pregnant and had to go to hospital [31] for Roy's boy friend. On Tuesday from Wednesday Roy had a friend. His name was Jamie Jessop. Jessop was his surname, like Marbella Jessop. His real name was [32] Jamie. His birthday was on the same day as Roy's but one thing – Roy was eight and Jamie was two. Soon Jamie caught up with Roy. They were both the [33] same age as Roy. One week passed and then Jamie went to school with Roy while Superstrong would lay the table and get everything ready for when Roy and Jamie came [34] back at 4.00 p.m. Marbella would come and take them home in their Rolls-Royce because they were famous and had lots of money. After that they had tea and went out to play football. After that they came in and had a little snack. Then they went to play with their toys. After that it was supper time.

Patrick was five-and-a-half years old when he began writing *Roy the Boy*. He had been attending school for some months without making much effort at writing, though his reading was well advanced and included, besides 'respectable' reading, several regular comics. He had earlier learned to type a little, and through the use of the space-bar, became aware of word spaces in written language. His manual dexterity with a pencil was one of many indications of unusual talent. He had learned to talk early in life and rapidly acquired a very large working vocabulary. He had also learned from his generous share of adult talk, a range of language functions which included story-telling: lengthy chunks of narrative were no problem to him. Indeed, when he read aloud it sounded like story-telling without a written version to read from.

Writing is a slow business, especially for young children. At first the difference in speed between thought and writing is overwhelming. For Patrick, however, the physical act of writing was not difficult: he wrote fast, without there being any great hindrance to his flow of ideas. Whenever he felt like writing, he took up whatever pen was handy and put on paper what he had already thought about. *Roy the Boy* was preceded by a longish fantasy about ancient (American-style) Rome entitled *Patsy out West*, and written in a large exercise book. Before this, there had been only snippets of writing.

The family had by this time travelled in France and Spain. They were all well-versed in map reading and camping techniques. The elements of these holiday experiences are to be found in *Roy the Boy*. Roy's mother is named Marbella after a Spanish town. Roy's father, however, is straight out of a comic with a good deal of manly magic about him. In spite of this *Roy the Boy* is a very domestic tale. Its substance is taken directly from first-hand experience. The early episodes concerning the aeroplane quickly give way to those related to Roy's birth and his frequent birthdays. His secure affectionate environment is clear from the way he writes about Roy at home – the twenty kisses to wake him up, his confidence at three years of age in the face of a ghost. He faces the destruction of his home in a fire with little concern, showing much more for the homeless condition of the family afterwards. Relief at being saved overwhelms regrets for what has been lost, and exemplifies the optimism with which Patrick views life. With school, we have the first mention of *work* which, whatever its nature, is so tiring that he has to go to bed on returning home. School is also the first occasion for sadness in an otherwise exhilarating, fast-moving story. But this is resolved by Marbella's gift of another son to Superstrong and thus a brother ('boy-friend') for Roy. This new character, Jamie Jessop, has magic birthdays too and soon reaches the same age as Roy; thus Roy's desire for a friend is fulfilled in his imagination.

He is a little muddled about the role Superstrong has: sometimes he is Marbella's husband, sometimes her father. But he is entirely successful in incorporating each new episode into the story, and in doing so he writes about happy family relationships and about some of the values, beliefs and attitudes he is acquiring. To get down on paper over 1000 words of narrative Patrick needed to have a firm grasp of spelling and hand-writing so that he could be quick, confident and more or less unhesitating. He also needed to be free to write when he felt like it, and to use his own ideas in his own way. It is important to note the differences between the privacy possible for him at home and the much more public nature of the classroom. On the few occasions when he asked for help with the spelling of a word, he got it. Those around him never commented about the quality of either his handwriting or his spelling. In fact he was never made to feel that anything he had done was 'wrong'. His story was accepted as something private, something which belonged to him. It was a record of his private thoughts, shared willingly with people among whom there was the greatest mutual respect. It was in such circumstances that *Roy the Boy* was completed.

Through his writing Patrick gives us a glimpse of his 'model of the world' and lets us see part of the 'state of his language' at this point in his life. We see his private meanings unfold as Roy grows from infancy to childhood and are made to realize how little we know of this private world, not because children are unwilling to tell us, but because we do not listen to them attentively or take them seriously enough. To be serious about children begins with acceptance of them in their own right.

5 Listening to Children

There is general agreement that children's language develops most rapidly between the ages of about eighteen months and four years, the pre-school years, when they spend most of their time at home. The influence of the home environment upon the development of children's language is clearly of the greatest importance.

From the research done by Dr Joan Tough of the University of Leeds it appears that differences in the language of children coming from different linguistic backgrounds can be seen at the age of three. In her analysis of the purposes for which three-year-old children in the study use language she found that:

(1) the children coming from 'unfavoured' groups used speech almost three times as often as the 'favoured' to secure attention for their own needs and to maintain their own status by defending or asserting themselves.
(2) the 'favoured' used language five times as often as the 'unfavoured' for extending or promoting action and for securing collaboration with others.
(3) the 'favoured' used language almost three times as often to convey information not apparent from the concrete situation.
(4) the 'favoured' used more than twice as much speech for the promotion of imaginative play and more than five times as much for creating imaginary situations out of the use of concrete materials.

It is difficult to define exactly what constitutes a 'favoured' or 'unfavoured' home background for a three-year-old. Nevertheless it is clear that environment is a critical factor in the development of language. That is why we keep insisting in environmental features and placing samples of children's language within the environment from which they arose.

We had already discussed certain aspects of the child's environment. Here we want to deal briefly with one important feature: *the adult's listening* to the child's language. It is extremely important for the adults who are part of a child's environment to be aware of his need not only to be talked to but also to be *listened to*. In the 'portraits' which precede this section we have two examples of high-quality adult listening: Nigel's parents and Stephen's mother. Obviously this does not mean that parents should rush about following their children with note-books or tape recorders. It means *knowing* the child's language and following its development. This knowledge of the child's language – his meanings, his own way of indicating his need to communicate and to convey information – is the basic requirement for linguistic interaction between adults and children and is reached essentially through *listening*.

The amount an adult listens directly to a child's language is firstly a clear indication of the quality of the care given to the child: it is revealing that the child coming from 'unfavoured' environments used language almost *three times* as often as those from the 'favoured' environments *to secure for their own needs* and *to maintain their own status by defending or asserting themselves*. There is no doubt that these children crave to be listened to and this craving is an indication of how little they have been listened to. Secondly, listening has a decisive influence on the socializing of the child: on the way they seek communication and interaction with others. The 'favoured' children used language *five times* as often as the 'unfavoured' for *extending or promoting action and for securing collaboration with others*. In listening to these children adults have responded in ways which satisfy the child's needs and encourage interaction with others.

The ability to convey information to express oneself and to make oneself understood are all vital for communication with others. This ability suffers greatly if a child is not listened to: the 'favoured' used language almost *three times* as often to convey information *not apparent from the concrete situation*. As it has been pointed out the remarkable linguistic ability of Patrick and Jonathan owes much to their linguistic interaction with people around them, thus to the seriousness with which they were listened to.

Language is a social act, a dialogue between participants who are both speakers *and* listeners. If one or other aspect is missing, this social act is broken. When a child is not listened to, he in turn is unable to learn *how* to listen and he will strive to be listened to in hopeless circumstances. Ignoring the child's language by not listening to it deprives him of the necessary partner in the linguistic act and this may well force him into silence or monologue. Listening is not a passive activity. Only by listening actively can an adult take up the subject matter of a child's communication and expression, and help him to extend his use of language.

It would be wrong to associate 'unfavoured' children with a single social class or to assume that they belong to a particular culture, a particular group of dialect speakers. It is equally mistaken to identify 'favoured' children with, for instance, middle-class children or the 'standard dialect'. There is no universal pattern of linguistic 'achievement' and *no* 'standard dialect' which must be mastered for a speaker to be considered a 'good' speaker. There are many patterns of achievement. There are also many dialects, all able to foster the ability to communicate with others and to convey information. That many people believe otherwise is part of social ideology, and social ideology and linguistic facts are obviously *not* the same matter.

6 Television and Comics

Television

Both television and comics have a strong influence upon many children and many parents are uncertain of the attitude they should take towards them.

Of the two, television is undoubtedly the most powerful. It is *the* medium of our technological era and is unrivalled for the amount of information it can make available in a few minutes from the most distant places. It is about television that parents ask questions of the kind: Should children watch television or not? How much? What kind of programmes? Can television influence children's language? Can they learn from television?

From a linguistic point of view the benefit of children watching television *on their own* is not very great. Even in cases where children spend more time watching television than in talking with their parents, it is the language of the home, not of television that is learned and used. Language learning requires feedback and this is only possible in life. Television produces speech and meanings of various kinds through pictures, language and other sounds. But television does not listen, respond, or acknowledge a particular viewer. When children talk about what they have experienced on television they talk as those in their environment do, not as television sets, though they may add new words to their vocabulary; in addition, because television casts its net widely and is in part the voice of the consumer society, indiscriminate viewing will include many 'voices' – some of which are as undesirable as the people from whom children are protected in real life.

But through watching television with adults, many opportunities for talking about what is viewed, for clarifying meanings and making discoveries may arise. For example, out of a programme on wild animal life watched and commented on together by child and adults much can be learned. In this case the television provides a *situation* for child–adult interaction and learning on the part of the child. The amount and the quality of what is learned is directly related to the quality of child–adult interaction, only indirectly to the programme viewed.

A child left on his own in front of a television set will not gain much experience or learning. In extreme cases too much solitary viewing may help to keep his mind blank by offering him a constant flow of images to consume passively on his own. If television as it is offered actually to the consumer could do linguistic 'miracles' – which it cannot – many difficult educational problems would already have been solved.

The second point about which parents feel concerned is *what kind* of programmes. Attitudes vary from complete indifference in which the child is allowed to watch anything he wants, to narrowly re- stricted attitudes where children are only allowed to see what is labelled 'children's programmes'. Here, as in the choice of books, parents have the responsibility to act according to their values and their beliefs. Of the two attitudes discussed above the first refers to people who seek to keep 'the children quiet' no matter how. The second may correspond to over-protective parents or those who are themselves unable to be critical. For all 'children's programmes' are not necessarily interesting; nor have they equally satisfactory peda- gogical contents. Sometimes they are dull, repetitive, stereotyped and boring and children's interest in them is likely to drop very quickly. Programmes with a carefully planned pedagogical content like *Sesame Street* for instance, are still rare – especially given the resources that could be made available.

Those who are guided simply by choosing children's programmes may miss a lot of good programmes out of which positive learning could arise. Here we have in mind a wide range of programmes which could be labelled 'reportages' on animals, wild life, natural parks, other societies, other cultures, other countries, other environments and ways of life (for instance a programme on Esquimos), the sea . . . numbers of programmes out of which talk, inquiries, discoveries, surprises, wonders and positive learning may take place if the right kind of adult interaction is provided. Other programmes – some- times adult favourites – must in any case be examined critically, for their overall inner structure is directed not to the child's mind, interests, understanding, language and expectations but to the adult's. Plots, happenings and motivations are beyond the child's experience and hence his understanding. Violence, murder and sadism should be discouraged for children *and* adults alike.

Comics

The comic strip is often looked upon as a minor genre in children's literature, the 'bastard' of the family. In fact there is nothing wrong with the comic-strip *technique*. It has been proved a highly successful way of telling stories in which pictures give the story a 'visual' narrative plot and brief 'speech balloons' illustrate the interactions of the characters in dialogue form. This has considerable advantages for children's learning, in particular for slow learners or those who need to visualize contexts before they are able to reach some level of abstraction. In fact the technique of comic-strip story-telling is a winner. In addition, because of its visual element the child's interest is often more long lived than in stories in which text is dominant. Some of the most interesting author-illustrators owe some features of their work to comic-strip techniques – Richard Scarry, for instance.

What should be more carefully considered is the contents of comic-strips, not the techniques themselves. Unfortunately many seem only to glorify violence: their contents vary narrowly from constant shooting and fighting to the glorification of war and the praise of crime. Needless to say these should be kept away from children.

Another kind of 'comics' show the everyday activities of children and animals. Those try to be 'funny' as well as instructive and usually combine their comic-strip pages with pages in which puzzles, pictures, games and information are given. These comics are of uneven quality. Some are very poor and only offer unimaginative and repetitive 'stories'. Some are more dignified and though they are not the most powerful pedagogical tool they are not harmful either. In any case the parent's choice is the decisive element. In deciding, they should bear in mind two points: firstly, fascination. Any pictures (and especially comic-strip pictures) have great fascination for young children: they are likely to be as fascinated by imaginative ones as by poor and dull ones. They go straight to the visual information, the characters, the details . . .

Secondly, though some parents look down on any kind of comic because it is a comic, many modern mythologies owe much to comic-strips and parental prejudices will not prevent their children from discovering the existence of this ubiquitous story-telling technique. Indeed comics are so widespread today that it is difficult to think how children could be kept in ignorance of them. This being so it is surely best for parents to promote comics which entertain and inform children in ways that are entirely in keeping with their interests, their understanding and their level of development. To ensure this, it is the content not the form of the comic which needs to pass muster.

7 Making Books at Home

Suggesting that books should be made at home may sound rather strange. Often when this suggestion is made we have heard disconcerted questions from parents: 'Is it really necessary for young children to have books?' 'Don't you think he or she is too young for books?' 'Does it mean that I should teach him to read?' Here we are not using the word book in the narrow sense as an 'object to be read' but in a much wider one: the book as a means of *conveying information*. As a beginner, exploring the world of his first-hand, immediate experience, the child needs to have available a great deal of information about this world. At the same time he needs to learn how to make sense of the pictures which offer him some of that information. In short, children need books in order to extend their awareness of the world and to enable them to reflect on the knowledge they are accumulating. But if this is to be possible, considerable help from adults will be necessary: help in learning how to 'see' pictures, how to inquire about pictures.

It is a serious mistake to think that little children can be given pictures to look at as if the pictures will explain themselves. This is very far from the truth. Until other people intervene in this process to explain the pictures and to guide the child in his searches, they will have little significance. The child put aside with a picture book of any kind quickly tires of it. He turns the pages this way and that, seeing very little because he cannot ask questions and hear someone talking to him about what he sees and wishes to understand. In these circumstances a picture book may be of as little value as a television set in promoting an interest in what is seen. The pictures are no more than a medium through which the child can reach out towards the real world – in the absence of this real world; and it is language shared with an adult which enables this to happen. The pictures are the starting points from which entirely new experiences may be had, but only when someone puts into words the reality that the pictures 'silently' symbolize.

Early in his life Nigel developed an interest in trains. He had little wooden ones to play with and real ones to experience when he was taken on journeys. At two he knew about steam trains and diesel trains; about carriages, wagons, freight carriers; about railway lines, signals, bridges and tunnels. He had begun to master the subject of trains through his first-hand experience in the company of adults who not only answered questions but who also gave him information he did not have access to. He learned a technical vocabulary related to trains and used this when he was going on a train journey, when he was watching trains and when he was looking at pictures of trains. He had two kinds of books about trains: one which was a photographic record of the age of the steam train and another which was home-made. The first was not addressed to children but because it was a serious study with splendid illustrations it had much more to offer than a book of 'nursery' trains. Nigel's 'nursery' trains were *objects* which his imagination transformed into real trains. They were controlled by him. They then became more than objects. They became *symbols* which he manipulated. Pictures of nursery trains were of less interest to him.

When his home-made book of trains was made it contained pictures of many kinds, but each was a picture of real objects in a real environment. From his extensive questioning and from all the talk about the train pictures, he knew not only about each train, but about the place it was in, the load it was carrying, the fuel it was burning; about its colour, its speed and about the men who made it go. Each picture became the focus for much speculation and, from putting together all the known facts, of much reasoning about the how, the why and the where of trains.

So, by the time he was two, Nigel knew about paper as an important material that made pictures and books possible. While his own scribbling was still non-representational he was delighted to sit and watch someone draw the train he had just been on. He would comment on the drawing critically, ask questions and propose additions which came to him from his own observation.

Nigel had some board-books with strong pages and washable pictures. With these he learned how to handle a book, how to turn the pages, how to hold it, and eventually, how to begin at the beginning and turn the pages one after another. Inevitably his interests took him towards books with paper pages because it was these in which he found what he responded to most strongly.

Although the subject of trains was an enduring interest, this was not the only one. He responded enthusiastically to the rhythm of music and speech, to rhymes and songs and to books of these. He liked listening to stories also. Sometimes he would ask for a story from a book but sometimes he wanted to be *told* the same story. His awareness of the difference between telling a story and reading a story arose from his early understanding that everyone can make up stories. He himself made up stories when playing with his toys – especially when he was on his own. He made up stories when looking at the home-made train book. He was told stories at bed time.

He also learned that some story-tellers write their stories down on paper. Once when his father was away from home, he wrote little stories to Nigel. Writing and its association with stories was becoming clear to him. But the need to have stories told and not read was still important. When stories were being told questions and speculations became part of the telling, part of an exploration of thinking and feeling exactly suited to him as the listener. In time, however, some stories became associated so closely with books and pictures, that the language of the book came to be accepted as special. He began to remember the text. Afterwards he would talk about characters and events, trying to understand what the story was about, asking endless questions, comparing events in one story with those in another.

Nigel's home-made book of trains, made from sheets of brown paper folded and stitched, was a record of his gradual accumulation of information about trains, stations, journeys, travel, places and people. The pictures which were pasted into it were taken from magazines and newspapers, from brochures and advertisements. Together these were investigated over and over again until the information they contained was familiar. Real and imaginary trains and journeys came together in the persistent questions and patient answers which began with the pictures and ended outside the pictures in accounts from the railway experiences of visitors who shared Nigel's book with him.

Sharing the book ('shall we look at this together?') was an invitation to answer questions, to tell stories about trains and train journeys, to give information and listen to what Nigel had to say on his own account. It was this interaction with people who knew and were willing to tell, that made the pictures come alive, and made their pictorial information available to him.

What can one make books of? Animal pictures almost certainly have a place. But there is also a place for a book with pictures of people, of faces, of crowds, of birds, of flowers, cars, boats, toys . . . Magazines contain many pictures suitable for home-made books. A more personal book (*Head, Body and Legs*) may be entirely devoted to details about the child and the people he knows. Pages in such a book might have photographs and early drawings; outline drawings of hands and feet; a picture of the child's face with labels for eyes, ears, nose, mouth; patterns of fingerprints and palmprints; pictures of feet; counting pictures with fingers and toes. The idea may be extended to include details of a dog or a cat or a pet budgerigar.

A texture and colour book may be made from odds and ends of materials. These are stuck on to the pages of a book to draw attention to the way things feel: rough and smooth fabrics, slippery plastic, rough sandpaper, scraps of leather, aluminium foil, string glued on paper in various patterns, and so on.

A seasons book will help to show the cycle of the year – especially as this affects town life where trees and flowers may well not be much in evidence and where sparrows and pigeons are present, like humans, all year round. Such a book might answer the question: 'How are the seasons experienced in towns?' Windy weather, snow, rain, dark and light, heat and cold, winter clothes, summer clothes, holidays, the return to school, visits to a park, birds nesting in houses, bird song, the changing patterns of light and dark, the sky, the new leaves on trees, a bulb growing in spring: all these and many more simple things of the way the year goes by will help the child to understand the constantly changing pattern of the seasons.

Adding Writing to Home-Made Books

Making books like these, and talking with children about them may well give rise to the request for some writing to be added to each page.

When Diane was four, she and her elder brother made books of big and little things. At first her brother simply wrote the words *big* or *little* under her pictures as appropriate. Then she herself dictated labels like: 'a big lady', 'a little girl' to whoever was available to write for her. Soon her brother taught her words like huge, tiny, enormous, microscopic (which she pronounced 'microsip'). In time she learned how to use these words and discovered that they are relative, that is, that their meanings are dependent on their contexts. Thus looking at a greenfly under a magnifying glass called for the word 'huger'. 'It's getting huger and huger,' she said. Then she added 'It has legs. It's walking.' Suddenly a monstrous greenfly appeared in her book. She could not have made this discovery on her own, but having been helped to make it, she then proceeded to make the experience her own. She also went on to discover other interesting facts about minute objects and creatures.

Diane's mother added neat, clear writing with a black felt pen to all Diane's attempts at writing. In this way Diane was reminded of the look of public writing. After some weeks she ignored her own writing and she readily accepted her mother's as the version to be read. She was, in this way, able to refine her visual memory of written words. She began to notice words she had seen in other books and her awareness of words in streets and shops increased. It would be wrong to give the impression that Diane was always reading. She led a very full life in which reading and writing had a small but growing place. She was made much more conscious of written language through picture story books than by any other means but her home-made books were an important part of all this because in them she was herself able to have a hand in making material for reading and writing and talking about.

Books made at home should be made in the simplest possible way. by folding large sheets of paper* in half and stapling or sewing them together securely. They should always begin with some interest the child has and should aim to deal with the child's personal exploration of familiar things. Much of the latter will not appear in the book, but will come out of the making of the pictures and out of the talking which will take place every time the book is looked at.

Diane's books were made regularly when the *idea* of making books

*Rolls of lining-paper used in paper-hanging are good for this.

was established. Here are some examples, including the writing Diane asked to have added to each page.

Diane's book

This contained six large pages of brown paper. It contained pictures and the following text:

I can count one two three four five
Little red riding hood
wolf go away
flowers for my nanny
I can count the petals
petals one petal two petals three

Sunday Book

We did have a picnic
a wasp on the jam
a huge wasp
I can nearly swim.
Daddy can swim
Mummy can swim
I can walk up the hill
Lambs are funny at running

Coloured leaves

In the autumn Diane collected leaves of varied shapes, sizes and colours. She drew round them and painted pictures and patterns. This book had less writing:

One leaf with some red
yellow on this
yellow and brown and yellow
red and orange
Kicking leaves about
try and catch a leaf.

Seagulls

Once Diane went to the sea. There she saw seagulls and was spellbound by the way they behaved when scraps of food were thrown into the water. She watched them snatch food out of the water. She saw them fly off. She saw them glide and land on the sea wall and on the masts of little boats. Later she was shown a book about seagulls and she recalled much of what she had seen. She painted pictures of seagulls afloat, seagulls in flight, and seagulls perched on the sea-wall. Her seagull book was quickly made because the impact of first-hand experience was so great.

a seagull in the sky
a seagull eating some bread
a seagull floating in the water
I love seagulls
Hundreds of seagulls
a seagull can walk on two legs
can I catch a seagull?
Seagulls
a boat and it has six seagulls on it
Baby seagulls with their mother

Diane made another bird book when she had no more to say about seagulls. She noticed sparrows and pigeons as she had never done before and made a book about them:

Sparrows are very little.
Quick. because of the cat
Get away, that cat will eat you up
Pigeon Why are pigeons so big?
Sparrows are made little.
Sparrows are very quick
Sparrows eating my crusts up.
Pigeons take things from sparrows
Wings, beak, claws, feathers.

In this book, Diane collected pigeon feathers and stuck them into the book. She could find no sparrow feathers. 'They're so small,' she said. 'They blow away I expect.'

Some people

Diane's picture of an old lady asleep was discovered after a year. She thought it was funny and wanted to do another. This began a book about people. Like all the others, each page of this book, with its picture (and often, but not always with writing), was the outcome of experience and questioning. The pictures were richly rewarding ways of putting together thoughts and impressions. The text was often no more than a label. But when the book was looked at afterwards, she recalled much of what each picture recorded and asked further questions – or perhaps the same questions all over again. Children often need to come back to the problem of understanding the answers to their questions.

Old people and babies were of great interest to Diane. She longed to hold babies in her arms and looked intently at babies in prams. Her pictures were simple records of her delight in people:

A little little baby.
A pram with two babies
two twin babies
A baby crying.
A little boy can walk.
Old lady and a baby out for a walk.

It is important to stress the part played by everyone around Diane (as with Nigel). Left to herself, Diane would not have produced books like these. But equally, if she had been forced into making books for the good of her soul, she would, in all likelihood, have done so with little enthusiasm. If her parents had interfered with her own natural way of doing this, the books would have been very different. And if there had been no talk, no questioning, no discussion, Diane would have been unfortunate indeed. Books like these were made as reflections on life while she was busy living it. 'Living it' was of first importance. Reflecting upon experience in the company of those around her was also important because of the deeper understanding that arose from *shared* experience.

Diane's books are therefore very personal. They reflect her world and snippets of her language. Whenever anyone helped her to write, great care was taken to write down what she had said. Early on, Diane had learned that if she spoke a great deal, expecting it all to be written down, people were likely to say: 'I can't write all that, Diane. There isn't room. Say the best bit.' She learned that it was wise to keep the best bit short; but it was always what *she* wanted.

When she came to look at the pages later, she would often go into great detail about her pictures to anyone sharing her book with her and *her* reading of the text was usually done after she had had the text read to her. There was never any suggestion that she had to read the books – as an exercise or as an occasion on which she could show off. Because of this, she had complete confidence in herself and no fear that she would be required to pass a test every time she opened one of her books. Talk always came first. Reading was incidental just as the original writing had been. In time, Diane remembered what she had written and began to recall words and phrases with accuracy. But had she *not* done so, impatient demands for her to do so would have done great harm. She would have ended by refusing to participate in looking at books because of the fear and confusion that would have been prompted in her.

8 The Importance of Stories for Children

The reading and telling of stories continued to be of great importance to Diane and Nigel. Each day was ended with stories. During the day rhymes and songs were sung and often, just before she went to sleep, Diane sang to herself. What was she learning from stories and pictures? In the broadest sense she was learning what life is about. She was viewing life through the information which writers, artists and photographers were offering to her. They took her by means of shared imagination into the lives of others, into places she could not visit, into the past and into make-believe. Through them she was able to share experiences and to come to an understanding of her own experiences through the medium of the printed word. In being read to she listened to all kinds of people using language in their own ways, people who had the power to move her to wonder or laughter, who helped her to understand her own feelings and those of other people, and hence to enlarge her sympathy for others; people who taught her about good fortune and misfortune, who set down accounts of the small wonders of the world for her to think about. But it was through the intervention of those around her, and through *their* familiar voices that writers emerged from the printed page to become established friends or just acquaintances.

Sometimes the family would quote little bits of a story; or sometimes a real person was seen to resemble a character in a book. Sometimes, as with the seagulls, there was a new experience of life to investigate and the right book made this possible in a remarkable way. Diane was learning that one of the great attributes of books is that they can be looked at, read and listened to just as the users wish – and as often as they want to. At the moment a book is taken from the shelf someone else's experience becomes available. As the pages are turned, it is unfolded.

When Diane listened to stories she was sometimes buried in bedclothes, sometimes sitting upright, but always near enough to see the pages and pause to look again and again at pictures, making sure that nothing had been missed. The pages turn; she watches the face of the reader; she notices the eyes move and the lips move. The story becomes part of her experience; the language of the story part of her language; its meanings part of the accumulating knowledge of people and of their attitudes and beliefs, their behaviour and their feelings, their characters and their actions. But all the while life at first hand is there to test a book against. For books are not substitutes for living.

Any consideration of children's literature is closely related to the wider and more general questions. What is literature? What does it do? Here we will define literature as a *medium* used to give a view of man and the world which surrounds him. In this sense literature is like a mirror which reflects man's life – his joys and sorrows, his problems and struggles, his hopes and values, his lies and mistakes. Literature also asks questions about reality, identity, about the 'sense' of the surrounding world in a way which usually has no place in everyday life in which there is little time for reflection.

The child too asks many questions – except if he has been trained to be silent and to swallow his desire for knowing – and not only questions about trains or animals, but also questions about life.

In order to discover what literature is – what it offers – the young reader needs a quiet place in which to be able to read, a corner of his own, and time to get involved in things that matter to him. The very young need to be close to an adult who will guide them into the meaning of books and stories. It is obvious that everybody is not equally responsive to literature and that everybody does not ask the same from literature. Unfortunately, there are some for whom books are of little importance. It is inevitable that the part literature plays in the lives of those in the child's environment will determine both the kind of introduction to literature they will give to the child, and the role the book will play in the child's development.

In the bibliographies which follow we have provided details of books of different kinds, for different age groups. We cannot make an exhaustive analysis of the contents and qualities of these books because this would require a lengthy book of its own. What we are saying is: 'This is part of what is available – an interesting part; the choice is yours.' Nevertheless some brief comments on children's literature may help your choice or may even help you to question the suitability of certain books.

It is very common for children's books to be judged only on the quality of the pictures. The text is very often overlooked. A quick survey of children's books will show that there are often far better illustrators and artists than writers. Often a mediocre and even a poor story is beautifully illustrated and this enables the book to 'look' good and to sell well. This is a matter which needs careful consideration. One solution is to use such a book just as a picture story book: to consider the pictures, to talk about them with the child and to make up a better story than the one actually printed.

One of the most important aspects to consider in children's books is the role of 'fantasy': what kind of fantasy, what kind of characters. Children should know that fantasy describes an imaginary, not a real world; no child should be drawn into a world of witches and fairies *without understanding that it is a make-believe world*, often a 'black' literary world. Our understanding of children has changed greatly but some children's books are printed and reprinted again and again, only the illustrations being changed. Even if plastic witches and monsters are now part of the toy industry, some of the 'good old stuff' may be harmful, as the following illustration shows.

Esther is a clever little girl who showed clear signs of intellectual curiosity from a very early age. She grew up confidently, asking many questions about life, and none was left without an answer, even if sometimes it was difficult to give one. Her parents and other adults around her spent time talking with her. No 'protective shell' was built round her. Her parents were highly selective in the books they chose – they were concerned to give her a valid picture of the world. If poor quality comic-strips got into her hands they were looked at and discussed critically with her. They had no television in the house, considering that more creative activities were preferable. But if she asked permission to go and see a programme with one of her friends it was always given. She grew up asking many questions, finding answers to some, but left sometimes with misunderstandings. She was full of confidence. Life was at times complicated, but slowly and progressively she was building a picture of the world, the *real world* which both surrounded her and was beyond her immediate environment.

When she was nearly six, she asked to have a holiday with her mother's aunt, for Esther lived in a flat and her mother's aunt had a big house and garden. As usually happened when she asked to spend a few days with friends or relatives, she was allowed to do so. The old lady started to tell Esther all the 'good old stuff' about witches and evil giants. During the first few days Esther refused to believe what she heard but the old lady insisted. To heighten the effect she used to make strange noises like cats in the garden to introduce a witch or an ogre. In only two weeks Esther passed from a world of confidence to a world of fear and uncertainty. She started to behave as though her previous understanding of the world had been destroyed: she refused to go to pick up a toy in her room on her own, she was upset when it got dark; she cried at night when she awoke; and she had a constant obsession with a menacing occult world which she thought she could see in the dark or whenever she was alone in a room for a few minutes.

The old lady was indignant and could not understand why Esther refused to see her again ('She's a witch,' Esther had told her mother one day). But the old lady was unable to accept that this 'old stuff' could be harmful to her grand-niece.

The 'darkness' – social and cultural – in which the old lady's grandmother had lived is no longer part of our society, which has its own and different darkness. Her stories belong to a society in which witches, ghosts and evil spirits (as well as good spirits) had a significance they lack in ours. The ways of these societies are no longer our ways.

The question which arises is: Has 'fantasy' a role today as it had one hundred years ago? Can it retain the same images, the same characters, the same events, the same stories, the same contexts? Or does the child of today need more contemporary material on which to fantasize and to interpret some of the 'dark' areas of life? Although this is an important matter we do not have a ready answer. Some recent children's literature begins to provide answers but more is needed and closer links between the child's world and children's literature have still to be established.

The many ways in which writers solve the question of how to tell stories for very young children include the powerful influence of illustrations. In the case of picture story books these play an integral part in the telling. Books such as *Rosie's Walk* by Pat Hutchins, *Where the Wild Things Are* by Maurice Sendak and the remarkable series of books written by Beatrix Potter are fine examples of the way in which artist-authors deal with subjects which appeal to all children. In all of these and in many other books (for instance Russell Hoban's *Frances* stories) animals are given important parts to play in depicting the problems of growing up, the behaviour of families, the activities of good and bad characters. The use of animals in these examples is dignified and truthful. Children are reassured and instructed indirectly by each author's placing of the human situation at one remove from the immediate world of the child.

However, the use of animals is no guarantee of an author's reliability. There are many books in which animals mimic sophisticated adult behaviour and sentimentalize the relationship they portray. In such books a poverty of imagination and insight leave children with nothing to stimulate their inquiries about the human values in which they are deeply interested.

The real problems of life – fear, anger, misunderstandings, joy, sadness, the danger, the pleasure and the distress of relationships – are all to be found in children's literature. Many authors deal sensitively with the perplexities children themselves face from day to day. It is from such authors that children are able to extend their understanding of themselves and of the meaning of life. New myths which interpret our own times have replaced those of the past: myths about race and colour, rich and poor all over the world, generosity and greed, political rights, technology, the nature of work and the quality of life, the changing forms of family life, parental and sibling affection, the young and the old. It is the responsibility of parents to choose carefully from both older and modern children's books those that help their children to an understanding of the society in which they will soon have parts to play.

The books in the lists have been selected to exemplify the qualities we have discussed. In the collaborations of authors and artists we have looked for representations of life with which children will themselves be able to identify. Fact, fictions, fantasy, imaginings, however an author has chosen to write, his work has been judged by the extent to which validity and suitability have been realized.

Throughout these lists we have been concerned with the content of each book and its relevance to the intellectual and emotional life of young children.

The book-lists which follow are divided into five sections. The first, Board Books, is intended only for the very young. The next four lists – Bed-Time Stories, Rhymes, Books To Look At and Talk About, and Picture Story Books 1 – overlap one with another in respect of the ages at which children will enjoy them; the age-limits apply only in a very general sense. Indeed we hope that some books from all these sections will be available to children as soon as they need more than board books. The final list Picture Story Books 2, is intended for children who have already started to go to school.

Board Books (six months to three years)

Some years ago, the earliest books for children were rag books and these may still be found. However, their content was (and is) frequently unsuitable and the illustrations crude and garish. These board books present the youngest age groups with books that are meant to be taken seriously. They will certainly not be damaged by biting and dropping but their purpose goes far beyond the need to provide indestructible pages: they are visually delightful and they represent careful attempts to depict objects and scenes in which children are genuinely interested. They are books in a very real sense.

The Child's Play Board Books
1. *Toys*, Child's Play, Parton, 1973.
2. *Animals*, Child's Play, Parton, 1973.
3. *Transport*, Child's Play, Parton, 1973.
4. *Plants and Animals*, Child's Play, Parton, 1973.

Simple, bright felt and canvas pictures for children from nine months to one-and-a-half years old.

ROBERT BROOMFIELD, *Baby Animal A.B.C.*, Bodley Head, London, 1965; Picture Puffin, Harmondsworth, 1968.
HILDE HEYDUCK-HUTH, *When The Sun Shines*, Burke, London, 1969.
HILDE HEYDUCK-HUTH, *In The Forest*, Burke, London, 1969.
HILDE HEYDUCK-HUTH, *In The Village*, Burke, London, 1969.
HILDE HEYDUCK-HUTH, *The Three Birds*, Burke, London, 1969.

Bright, clear pictures with text in very large type and pages made strong enough to withstand every nursery activity. Excellent books to begin looking at and listening to – even with sticky fingers (the pages can be sponged clean). They will easily withstand any child's urge to eat them. The dog will not make much of them either.

Bed-Time Stories for Very Young Children

The secret of story reading lies in the way the reader is able to bring the listener and the writer together. It is the familiar voice, the closeness of reader and listener, the ability of the reader to be unobtrusively expressive which will help the child to interpret the story in his own way. It is important that the reader does not read too fast and that time is given to looking at the pictures and talking about them.

When a story becomes a great favourite, there may be many requests for it to be re-read. This may be simply for the sheer pleasure it affords the listener and it will require patience of any parent who is tired of hearing any particular book, to hear it over and over again. Occasionally there may have to be an agreed 'last time' after which a new story is to be introduced. However, children also ask to have a story repeated because they know they have not understood it completely. Each new reading enables them to grasp more and more detail and thus more and more of its meaning.

RUTH AINSWORTH (illustrated by Shirley Hughes), *The Ruth Ainsworth Book*, Heinemann, London, 1970.

A collection of this author's stories for the very young, including some old favourites (*Rufty Tufty*, for example) and some that are new. All the stories are very short.

RICHARD BAMBERGER (editor, translated by James Thin, illustrated by Emanuela Wallenta), *My First Big Story Book*, Young Puffin, Harmondsworth and Baltimore, 1969.

A collection of popular English nursery rhymes and bed-time stories mixed with some from other countries.

LEILA BERG (illustrated by Peggy Fortnual), *Little Pete Stories*, Young Puffin, Harmondsworth, 1959; Verry, Mystic (Conn.), 1964.

Little Pete is a four year old who plays on his own most of the time. Like all four year olds he is curious about the ordinary things of life which are often mysterious and new. He is also a thinker trying to understand the grown-up world. The author has a sharp ear for the quality of real conversations.

EILEEN COLWELL (compiler, illustrated by Charlotte Hough), *Time For A Story* (two- to four-year-olds), Young Puffin, Harmondsworth and Baltimore, 1967.

EILEEN COLWELL (compiler, illustrated by Judith Bledoe), *Tell Me A Story* (three- to five-year-olds), Young Puffin, Harmondsworth and Baltimore, 1962.

EILEEN COLWELL (compiler, illustrated by Gunvor Edwards), *Tell Me Another Story* (four- to six-year-olds), Young Puffin, Harmondsworth and Baltimore, 1964.

A mixture of verses, finger games and stories for very young children collected by a famous story-teller.

DOROTHY EDWARDS (illustrated by Henrietta Garland), *My Naughty Little Sister*, Young Puffin, Harmondsworth, 1963.

These stories were originally told to children before they were written down. This is perhaps why they sound so good to read aloud.

Also by DOROTHY EDWARDS (illustrated by Una J. Place), *My Naughty Little Sister's Friends*, Young Puffin, Harmondsworth, 1968; (illustrated by Shirley Hughes), *When My Naughty Little Sister Was Good*, Young Puffin, Harmondsworth, 1973.

BARBARA KER WILSON, *A Story To Tell*, J. G. Miller, London, 1964.

Thirty very short stories for children from two years old. Some four- and five-years-old will still enjoy them at bedtime.

Books of Rhymes

In recent years teachers in infant schools have discovered that large numbers of children come to school not knowing nursery rhymes.

This means that these children have not been sung to and have not heard rhymes. This is likely to indicate a pattern of upbringing that ignores important learning possibilities for the child. Nursery rhymes belong to a stage of childhood in which children are engaged in intensive language learning, learning about the world *through* language.

Nursery rhymes have grown out of an orally transmitted culture which used the power of imagination and of fantasy to great effect and language that exploits brilliant approaches to learning. Nursery rhymes deal with many of the interests young children have. With their help children may learn the parts of the body, names of the letters of the alphabet, the days of the week, to count and much more besides – all in a way which is imaginative and pleasurable and which demonstrates that words and ideas can be played with in surprising and delightful ways.

But more than this, nursery rhymes reflect the range of moods young children experience and life, death, love, marriage as well as violence (of the kind children know from time to time when they pass through a period of tantrums) are all plainly dealt with.

In the selection of books which follows additional pleasure is gained from fine illustrations.

FOR THREE- TO FIVE-YEAR-OLDS

TRUDE ALBERTI, *The Animal's Lullaby*, Bodley Head, London, 1967.

A gentle book based on an Icelandic lullaby told here in rhyme. Pictures of young birds and animals asleep and at the end, a baby who is being sung to.

LEILA BERG (compiler, illustrated by Shirley Burke and Marvin Bileck), *Four Feet and Two*, Puffin, Harmondsworth and Baltimore, 1960.

A collection of verses about animals of all kinds, some well-known poems and some that may be new to parents and children alike.

PAUL GALDONE, *Old Mother Hubbard and Her Dog*, Bodley Head, London, 1961; McGraw-Hill, New York, 1960.

After she went to the cupboard, where did Mother Hubbard go?

This book presents the whole nursery rhyme. The dog is modelled on the artist's own dog.

ELIZABETH MATTERSON (compiler, with diagrams by David Woodroffe), *This Little Puffin* . . ., Young Puffin, Harmondsworth and Baltimore, 1969.

A book of traditional songs, action-rhymes and musical games with instructions for playing them. Music, where it is part of the activity, is also provided.

NORAH MONTGOMERIE (illustrated by Margery Gill), *This Little Pig Went to the Market*, Bodley Head, London, 1966; Watts, New York, 1967.

A book of action rhymes for the very young, with instructions on how to perform each rhyme.

RODNEY PEPPÉ (compiler and illustrator), *Hey Riddle Diddle*, Kestrel Books (formerly Longman Young Books), Harmondsworth, 1971; Holt, Rinehart and Winston, New York, 1971.

A selection of traditional rhyming riddles humorously illustrated in colour.

VIRGINIA A. TASHJIAN (illustrated by Victoria de Larrea), *Juba This and Juba That*, Kestrel Books (formerly Longman Young Books), Harmondsworth, 1971.

A bumper book of songs and verses and singing games for children of three to five years. There are full illustrations on how the adult presents the activities. There are many orange-coloured pictures to illustrate the text.

BRIAN WILDSMITH (compiler and illustrator), *Mother Goose*, Oxford University Press, Oxford, 1964; Watts, New York, 1965.

Familiar rhymes accompanied by generous high-spirited pictures in the colourful Wildsmith style.

FOR FOUR- TO EIGHT-YEAR-OLDS

BARBARA and E. EMBERLY, *Drummer Hoff*, Bodley Head, London, 1970; Prentice-Hall, Englewood Cliffs, 1967.

The story of how an old-fashioned cannon is brought piece by piece to nowhere in particular, by Drummer Hoff, Private Parriage, Corporal Farrell and others. The cumulative verses describe it all in a mock-serious manner and the pictures ingeniously match the abrupt, wooden doings of these splendidly uniformed soldiers. The book ends with a splendid bang, the twisted cannon becomes a home for hedge sparrows and the countryside begins to grow over and hide the results of the explosion. What happened to Drummer Hoff and the others is left to the imagination.

RODNEY PEPPÉ *The House That Jack Built*, Kestrel Books (formerly Longman Young Books), Harmondsworth, 1970; Delacorte, New York, 1970.

A version with beautiful pictures and a special curtain-call of all the characters at the end.

BEATRICE SCHENK DE REGNIERS (illustrated by Beni Montresor), *Willy O'Dwyer Jumped in the Fire*, Collins, London, 1970; Atheneum, New York, 1968.

A nonsense rhyme about a boy who 'jumped into the . . .'. Each page ends with a jolt. But turn over and it all makes rumbustious sense as Willy goes from the fire into the pot, and so on. Then he goes all the way back.

Also by the same author and illustrator, *May I Bring a Friend?*, Collins, London, 1966; Puffin, Harmondsworth, 1972; Atheneum, New York, 1964.

A small boy takes a strange assortment of friends to have tea with a king and queen.

PETER SPIER, *The Erie Canal*, World's Work, Tadworth, 1971; Doubleday, Garden City, 1970.

The American folk-song about the canal from Albany to Buffalo. Set in 1850 Peter Spier's pictures depict in rich detail the journey the song commemorates. The music is included at the end of the book.

Also by PETER SPIER, *The Fox Went Out on a Chilly Night*, World's Work, Tadworth, 1962; Doubleday, Garden City.

Each stage in the fox's late night adventures is depicted with a wonderful sense of atmosphere. The countryside through which the fox travels is evoked in pictures full of beautiful detail.

London Bridge is Falling Down, World's Work, Tadworth, 1968; Doubleday, Garden City, 1967.

The familiar nursery rhyme is accompanied by fine pictures which have fascinating details about the collapse and possible methods of repairing the old bridge. There are also some dramatic incidents depicted with visual zest. Architectural problems and building methods are brilliantly recorded on Peter Spier's imaginative pages.

CAROL TATE, *Rhymes and Ballads of London*, Blackie, Glasgow, 1971; Scroll Press, New York, 1973.

Twenty-five traditional London rhymes and ballads with bright lively illustrations.

Books to Look At and Talk About

The books in this section are first and foremost *visual* books. They convey information or tell a story primarily through pictures. The text, where it does exist, is of secondary importance. They all provide opportunities for talk. They are not books to keep children quiet but to stimulate their questions. Depending on the answers they receive, the books will be more or less valuable as a way of learning about the world.

ERIC CARLE, *Do You Want to be My Friend?*, Hamish Hamilton, London, 1971; T. Y. Crowell, New York, 1971.

A mouse follows one tail after another – none belonging to very friendly owners – until he finds one just like his own.

JOHN S. GOODALL, *Jacko*, Macmillan, London, 1971; Harcourt Brace Johanovich, New York, 1972.

Jacko is a pet monkey who stows away aboard an eighteenth-century battleship. There is an exciting battle with a pirate ship and eventually, after much mischief, Jacko is able to return home. The pages are designed in an intriguing way so that half pages change one incident into another.

TANA HOBAN, *Look Again*, Hamish Hamilton, London, 1972; Macmillan, Riverside, 1971.

This book by the author of *Count and See* will help children to make all kinds of discoveries among familiar objects.

L. A. IVORY, *Rain*, Burke, London, 1970.
L. A. IVORY, *Sunshine*, Burke, London, 1970.
L. A. IVORY, *In the Street*, Burke, London, 1970.
L. A. IVORY, *At the Shops*, Burke, London, 1970.

A series intended for use at home with very young children. The simple text is modelled on the child's spoken language and suggests how the child should be encouraged to start talking about the pictures.

IELA and ENZO MARI, *The Egg and the Chicken*, A. & C. Black, London, 1970; Pantheon, New York, 1970.

IELA and ENZO MARI, *The Apple and the Butterfly* (Title in U.S.A.: *The Apple and The Moth*), A. &. C. Black, London, 1970; Pantheon, New York, 1970.

These books show the mysterious unseen processes by which a chicken is born and grows up, and how an egg laid in apple blossom becomes a butterfly. Diagrammatic pictures to which children and parents will wish to add the words for themselves.

ANTONELLA BOLLIGER-SAVELLI, *The Knitted Cat*, Hamish Hamilton, London, 1972.

The knitted cat is grey- and black-striped right down the tip of his tail – except that the last stripe is not finished off. A curly end of wool sticks out from it and this gives the mouse an idea. He pulls the wool and unknits a large part of the cat's fine tail. However, a visit to wise owl solves the problem. Bold, colour illustrations in collage reminiscent of some film cartoons.

RICHARD SCARRY, *What Do People Do All Day?*, Collins, London, 1968; Random House, New York, 1968.

A huge book in which nursery animals demonstrate how humans spend their time. The author-illustrator uses refined 'comic' technique to provide a vast range of information. There is a curiously successful blend of fantasy and reality in most pages and a strong sense of humour is never far off. Preschool children will soon become deeply absorbed in the detailed drawings of how a house is built, how coal is mined, how cloth is woven etc. Not a book to borrow nor one that can be looked at without an adult to help answer the questions that will arise.

Also by RICHARD SCARRY, *Great Big School House*, Collins, London, 1969; Random House, New York, 1969; *Great Big Air Book*, Random House, New York, 1971; *Best Word Book Ever*, Hamlyn, Feltham, 1970; Western Publishing New York, 1963.

MARION WALTER (illustrated by Narah Haber-Smith), *This is Annette*, André Deutsch, London, 1971; M. Evans, New York, 1972.
   A simple text with questions and puzzle illustrations to which the metal mirror in the cover supplies answers.

Also by MARION WALTER, *Make a Bigger Puddle, Make a Smaller Worm*, André Deutsch, London, 1971; M. Evans, New York, 1972.

BRIAN WILDSMITH, *The Circus*, Oxford University Press, London, 1970; Watts, New York, 1970.
   A glowing, resplendent circus in action, involving clowns and acrobats, balancing feats, fancy horseriding, lions, tigers, elephants and a marvellous assembly of forty gymnasts forming a vast pyramid that disappears beyond the page, all without a jot of audience and much nicer than life.

Also by BRIAN WILDSMITH, *Puzzles*, Oxford University Press, London, 1970; *Fishes*, Oxford University Press, London, 1968; Watts, New York, 1968; *Birds*, Oxford University Press, London, 1967; Watts, New York, 1967; *Wild Animals*, Oxford University Press, London, 1967; Watts, New York, 1967.

DENNIS WRIGLEY, *The Cog; The Lever; Sand; Sound; Speed; Water; The Wheel*, Lutterworth Press, Guildford, 1971.
   Simple scientific facts with fine simple line drawings which are clear and brightly coloured.

Picture Story Books 1 (Ages Three to Six)

JOHN BURNINGHAM, *Mr Gumpy's Outing*, Jonathan Cape, London, 1970; Holt, Rinehart & Winston, New York, 1971.

Page by page Mr Gumpy's boat fills with a fine assortment of creatures. Each asks 'May I come, please Mr Gumpy?' and is given permission if they promise not to do their 'thing' – like the pig for example: 'Very well, but don't muck about.' A watery end to the outing but a fine tea at the end of it. Fine illustrations.

VIRGINIA LEE BURTON, *Choo Choo; The Story of a Little Engine Who Ran Away*, Faber Paperbacks, London, 1971; Scholastic Book Services, New York, 1971.

A classic story about a steam train that runs away for a time and then returns home.

PHILIP D. EASTMAN, *Are You My Mother?*, Collins, London, 1972; Beginner Books, New York, 1960.

A baby bird has just hatched out but while his mother goes in search of food, he sets off to find her. He inquires of many strange 'mothers' before he finds her. A humorous story with simple but eloquent illustrations.

BENJAMIN ELKIN, *The Six Foolish Fishermen*, Brockhampton Press, London, 1958; Scholastic Book Services, New York.

Counting to six and including yourself may be harder than it is thought to be but nobody will ever feel as foolish making such a mistake as these six fishermen. A story with well devised repetitive passages.

MARY GARELICK (photographed by Rena Jakebsen), *What's Inside*, Scholastic Book Services, New York, 1970.

A photographic record of a chick hatching out. A realistic portrayal of birth with all elements of struggle clearly shown.

MARIANNE GERLAND-EKEROTH (photographed by Gosta Nordin), *My Own Little Cat*, Angus and Robertson, London, 1965; Coward, New York, 1963.

Sooby the cat has six kittens. Their growing up is observed by a little girl. Superbly photographed in black and white.

ANITA HEWETT (illustrated by Robert Broomfield), *Mrs Mopple's Washing Line*, Bodley Head, London, 1966; Picture Puffin, Harmondsworth, 1970.

A gentle story about the way the wind blew Mrs Mopple's washing around the farmyard. Each piece lands on an unsuspecting animal. Young children find it very funny.

RUSSELL HOBAN (illustrated by G. Williams), *A Baby Sister for Frances*, Faber, London, 1970; Harper-Row, New York, 1963; *Bedtime for Frances*, Faber, 1969; Harper-Row, New York, 1960; *Bread and Jam for Frances*, Faber, London, 1966; Harper-Row, New York, 1964.

These stories are about some of the awkward and downright difficult moments of childhood. They illustrate with tenderness and imagination that when these are dealt with patiently and with understanding, the problems may be resolved. The author's deep understanding of childhood is expressed through events in the lives of a family of badgers.

ADELAIDE HOLL (illustrated by Roger Duvoisin), *The Rain Puddle*, Bodley Head, London, 1966; Picture Puffin, Harmondsworth, 1970; Lothrop, New York, 1965.

When a hen looks into the rain puddle she thinks she sees a hen who will drown if she's not rescued. She goes off to find the turkey who looks into the puddle and thinks a turkey needs to be rescued. The turkey fetches a pig, the pig a sheep, the sheep a cow. But just then the sun comes out and the danger of drowning is over. A marvellous joke for four-year-olds, told with a very straight face.

PAT HUTCHINS, *Rosie's Walk*, Bodley Head, London, 1968; Picture Puffin, Harmondsworth, 1970; Macmillan, New York, 1971.

Rosie the hen goes for a walk before supper. A fox follows her as she goes 'round the pond, past the mill, over the hay cock' and at each stage he is halted from pouncing on Rosie by a fortunate disaster. Thanks to the bees, Rosie gets back in time for supper. A book very young children come to love. The pictures are jaunty and elegant and full of straight-faced comic situations.

Also by PAT HUTCHINS, *The Surprise Party*, Bodley Head, London, 1970; Picture Puffin, Harmondsworth, 1972; Macmillan, New York, 1972.

Rabbit decides to have a party and the news is passed on from one creature to another with very curious results.

BARBARA IRESON, *The Gingerbread Man*, Faber, London, 1968.

The gingerbread man is a jaunty character who gives everyone a good chase – except the crafty fox who carries him out of reach of his pursuers – almost to the other side.

CHIHIRO IWASAKI, *A Brother For Momoko*, Bodley Head, London, 1970.

Beautiful dreamy pictures and a text which is filled with tenderness for the new baby which has just arrived. A beautifully produced book.

Also by CHIHIRO IWASAKI, *Momoko's Lovely Day*, Bodley Head, London, 1969.

EZRA JACK KEATS (illustrated by the author), *Peter's Chair*, Bodley Head, London, 1968; Picture Puffin, Harmondsworth, 1973; Harper-Row, New York, 1969.

The jealousy felt by first born children when a baby arrives is the subject of this story. It is handled with delicacy and understanding by the author. The pictures are made with bright flat paint, collage and patterned paper.

JACK KENT, *The Fat Cat*, H. Hamilton, London, 1972; Picture Puffin, Harmondsworth, 1974; Parents Magazine, New York, 1971.

Translated from a Danish folk tale about an old woman and her cat. When she asks the cat to watch her porridge while it cooks, the cat eats first the porridge, then the pot, and then the old woman herself. Everything the cat encounters is eaten while he gets fatter and fatter . . . But there is a happy ending.

FELICITE LEFEVRE (illustrated by Tony Sarg), *The Cock, the Mouse and the Little Red Hen*, Bles, London, 1968; Dufour, Chester Springs, 1959.

The Cock is bad-tempered, the Mouse is lazy, the Little Red Hen hard-working and resourceful. They live together in a little house in which Little Red Hen does most of the work. When the fox catches all three and carried them off in a sack, all looks bleak. Only by working together and helping the Little Red Hen to engineer their escape are they saved from becoming the fox family's supper. The book has some delightful pictures and some that speak eloquently of the real danger in which the three animals find themselves. This 1907 version of the story is still the best available.

MARGARET MAHY (illustrated by Jenny Williams), *A Lion in the Meadow*, Picture Puffin, Harmondsworth, 1972; Watts, New York, 1969.

When you pretend, lions can be found in a quite ordinary meadow and they play with you – even when mother pretends that a dragon is in the next meadow. A beautiful concoction of reality and fantasy which shows what would happen if make-believe came true.

LETITIA PARR (photographed by Geoffrey Parr), *Seagull*, Angus & Robertson, London, 1970.

A poetic description in words and pictures of seagulls as they take off from the sea, fly overhead, flap and tilt in the wind and land with precision wherever they like. Together, pictures and text give a faithful and imaginative account of seagulls.

MAURICE SENDAK, *Where the Wild Things Are*, Bodley Head, London, 1967; Picture Puffin, Harmondsworth, 1970.

When Max is sent to bed his mother calls him a wild thing. All alone with his wildness, Max journeys to where other more fantastic wild things than he swing from trees, dance and shout and proclaim him king. As he calms them of their wildness, his own quiet self returns so he leaves them and sails back to his room where his supper is waiting for him – and it's still warm. There never were more cuddly, likeable, mildly awful monsters than those which fill the centre pages of this book. A classic picture story book.

MAURICE SENDAK and CHARLOTTE ZOLOTOV, *Mr Rabbit and the Lovely Present*, Picture Puffin, Harmondsworth, 1971. (In U.S.A. CHARLOTTE ZOLOTOV, *Mister Rabbit and the Lovely Present*, Harper-Row, New York, 1962.)

A beautiful book in all senses of the word and a classic of its kind. A perfect way to learn about colours, about presents and people. The writing has the quality of a folk tale shaped by years of story-telling.

ESPHYR SLOBÓDKINA, *Caps for Sale*, World's Work, London, 1960; Addison-Wesley, Reading, 1947.

A peddler who goes to sleep under a tree full of monkeys wakes to find all his caps gone. He soon finds out where they've gone and by accident he gets them all back.

WILLIAM STOBBS, *Henny-Penny*, Bodley Head, London, 1968; Picture Puffin, Harmondsworth, 1972; *The Story of the Three Bears*, Picture Puffin, Harmondsworth, 1971; *The Story of the Three Little Pigs*, Bodley Head, London, 1965; Picture Puffin, Harmondsworth, 1968.

Three stories which are enduring favourites with all children, boldly illustrated but so that the threatening elements in the stories are not too frightening. Stobbs' birds are especially well depicted.

Also by WILLIAM STOBBS, *The Three Billy Goats Gruff*, Bodley Head, 1967; McGraw-Hill, New York, 1968.

A frightening troll sits under the bridge and threatens the lives of all three Billy Goats Gruff. They are too wily for him however and they reach the grass on the other side of the valley by excusing their size and pandering to his greed. Strong supporting illustrations.

Picture Story Books 2 (Ages Five to Eight)

MICHAEL BOND (illustrated by Hans Helweg), *The Tales of Olga da Polga*, Young Puffin, Harmondsworth, 1971.

Olga da Polga is a delightful guinea pig and an enthusiastic seeker after adventure. She has an air of independence which many children will recognize in themselves.

ROBERT BROWNING, *The Pied Piper of Hamelin*, Faber, London, 1967.

The story of the rats, the mayor and the children of Hamelin illustrated with a fine medieval flavour.

JOHN BURNINGHAM, *Harquin: The Fox Who Went Down to the Valley*, Jonathan Cape, London, 1967; Bobbs-Merrill, Indianapolis, 1968.

A fox family is faced with disaster. The hunt are about to seize them one and all. Harquin leads the horses and the dogs into the mire to save his family. The squire ends up stuck fast in the mud. Strong dark pictures which capture the action and the mood of the story splendidly.

VIRGINIA LEE BURTON (illustrated by the author), *Mike Milligan and His Steam Shovel*, Faber, London, 1967; Houghton Mifflin, New York.

After a long useful life 'digging together for years and years', Mike Milligan and his steam shovel Mary Ann are overtaken by bigger and better mechanical shovels. He cannot face leaving her in the junk yard – and at last takes on a job for a wager and wins a new home for them both. Lively pictures by the author.

Also by VIRGINIA LEE BURTON, *The Little House*, Faber, London, 1968; Houghton Mifflin, New York.

The 'progress' of urban society is shown in the way the little house, once out in the country, becomes an awkward bit of a great city. All the changes this causes are presented with clarity. The happy ending is symbolic of the 'back to the countryside' longing many people now have.

ROALD DAHL, *Fantastic Mr Fox*, Allen & Unwin, London, 1970; Young Puffin, Harmondsworth, 1974.

Usually Mr Fox is the villain of the story. Here, in the opening pages, his home is broken into and he has to escape with his family – to all sorts of adventures – after which he doesn't seem so bad.

Also by ROALD DAHL, *James and the Giant Peach*, Puffin, Harmondsworth, 1973; Knopf, New York, 1961.

MARJORIE FLACK (illustrated by Kurt Wiese), *The Story about Ping*, Bodley Head, London, 1935; Picture Puffin, Harmondsworth, 1968; Viking Press, New York, 1933.

A yellow duckling called Ping lives in China with his mother and father and a very large family of brothers, sisters, uncles, aunts and cousins. He runs away and is stolen by a boy whose family intends to eat him. But Ping escapes and returns to his family, despite the punishment he ran away from in the first place. A story told with repeated phrases which young children love to contribute to. The gentle moral does not escape them.

WANDA GAG, *Millions of Cats*, Faber, London, 1929; Coward, New York, 1938.

The story of a lonely old couple who long to have children, and find 'hundreds of cats, thousand of cats, millions and billions of cats' instead. Page by page the number of cats grows larger and larger as the simple repetitive story unfolds.

PAT HUTCHINS, *Tom and Sam*, Bodley Head, London, 1969; Picture Puffin, Harmondsworth, 1972; Macmillan, New York, 1968.

Tom and Sam, once friends, spend their days outdoing each other in cleverness until they finally decide to end their rivalry and become friends again.

Also by PAT HUTCHINS (illustrated by the author), *Clocks and More Clocks*, Bodley Head, London, 1970; Picture Puffin, Harmondsworth, 1974; Macmillan, New York, 1973.

How do you know if a clock is telling the time correctly? In this story a house gets more and more marvellous clocks. Some children will begin to understand about telling the time by following Pat Hutchins' witty pictures.

CHARLES KEEPING (illustrated by the author), *Through the Window*, Oxford University Press, London, 1970; Watts, New York, 1970.

This author-artist is concerned to explore the moments of pain which sometimes afflict us all. Here, through the window of a small, rather dark room, a child looks out at the street and sees a dog killed by horses that suddenly bolt. A sad story in which a moving vision of reality is presented uncompromisingly.

Also by CHARLES KEEPING, *Charley, Charlotte and the Golden Canary*, Oxford University Press, London, 1967; Watts, New York, 1968; *Alfie and the Ferryboat*, Oxford University Press, London, 1968; *Shaun and the Cart-horse*, Oxford University Press, London, 1966; *Joseph's Yard*, Oxford University Press, London, 1969; Watts, New York, 1969.

Here also the stories and the illustrations break with traditional subject matter and explore contemporary life with unusual power. Each is a deeply serious study in which joy, sorrow and separation are handled with great skill. The mystery of a situation is conveyed by the strange and visionary pictures.

ASTRID LINDGREN (illustrated by Harald Wiberg), *The Tomten*, Kestrel (formerly Longman Young Books), Harmondsworth, 1962.

A book for a dark winter night, when in warmth and security, the story of the little troll who watches over animals and children will bring a sense of peace to reader and listener alike. The dark pictures of the northern landscape and the shadowy interiors of houses conjure up the quietness of the night. One can feel the friendly silence as the Tomten goes about his business.

DAVID MCKEE (illustrated by the author), *Mister Ben – Red Knight*, Picture Puffin, Harmondsworth, 1972; McGraw-Hill, New York, 1968.

A 'magic' story in which Mr Benn has some very unusual adventures which begin when he chooses a certain costume to wear to a fancy dress party. As soon as he puts on the Red Knight's splendid armour, strange things happen to him. The pictures are bold and exciting.

HELEN MORGAN (illustrated by Shirley Hughes), *Mother Farthing's Luck*, Faber, London, 1971.

Mother Farthing is an old woman who makes pies by magic. As she uses up eggs, new ones appear and when her milk jug is empty, it is filled up again. The little man who works magic on her behalf is Satchkin Patchkin. But Mother Farthing has an envious neighbour who is very suitably called Jasper Dark and he is out to take her magic for himself. Listening to the story, a child will soon be drawn to join in whenever the author uses her intriguing rhymes.

EVALINE NESS, *Sam, Bangs and Moonshine*, Bodley Head, London, 1967; Holt, Rinehardt & Winston, New York, 1966.

A prize-winning picture story book which tells of a child who 'tells stories'. Samantha is a 'story-teller' who said her mother was a mermaid. But this was really all moonshine.

PAMELA OLDFIELD (illustrated by Carolyn Dinan), *Melanie Brown Goes to School*, Faber, London, 1970.

Stories about a little girl's early days at school which may help children about to start school to understand what is it all about. Melanie not only wants to be helpful to her teacher, but insists on being so. She is full of enthusiasm and self-confidence. The author makes gentle fun of her.

PHILIPPA PEARCE (illustrated by Dereck Collard), *The Squirrel Wife*, Kestrel (formerly Longman Young Books), Harmondsworth, 1971; T. Y. Crowell, New York, 1972.

'Once upon a time, long ago, on the edge of a great forest, there lived two brothers who were swineherds. The elder brother was very unkind to the younger brother called Jack; he made him do all the work and gave him hardly enough to eat.' In this first paragraph of a new fairy story, the author casts her spell over the listener. The author's prose has all the qualities of a story which has itself come from a magical source. It sounds like an old, old story and yet she gives it a quality which is entirely of her own making. Beautiful illustrations.

CELESTINO PIATTI, *The Happy Owls*, Benn, London, 1965; Atheneum, New York, 1964.

The Happy Owls are wise and beautiful in this slender story of how contentment escapes the quarrelsome barnyard fowls. The brilliant pictures outshine this rather dull text.

BEATRIX POTTER (illustrated by the author), *The Tale of Peter Rabbit*, Warne, London, 1902; Mulberry Press, New York, 1967.

Against a delicately painted picture of the English countryside,

Beatrix Potter sets her stories of native animals. These reflect English life at the turn of the century. In her writing she never writes 'down' to children. Her imagination and her power to use real life situations come together in storytelling of a unique quality.

Also by BEATRIX POTTER (illustrated by the author): *The Tale of the Flopsy Bunnies*; *The Tale of Mrs. Tiggy-Winkle*; *The Tale of Squirrel Nutkin*; *The Tailor of Gloucester*; *The Sly Old Cat*; *The Tale of Jemima Puddle-Duck*; Warne, London; Mulberry Press, New York.

OTFRIED PREUSSLER (translated by Anthea Bell, illustrated by F. J. Tripp), *The Robber Hotzenplotz*, Abelard-Schuman, London and New York, 1965.

Large type and many funny pictures suggest this book as one which may first be read to children and then used to introduce them to reading. The story is about cops and robbers and its rather wild humour will motivate some children to tackle the book for themselves – with a bit of help to begin with.

ALF PRYSON (translated by Marianne Helweg, illustrated by Bjorn Berg), *Little Old Mrs Pepperpot*, Young Puffin, Harmondsworth, 1961; Astor-Honor, Stanford, 1960.

If you suddenly shrank to the size of a pepperpot at unexpected moments, if you were old, not very pretty but a resourceful comic, you would know exactly what the odd heroine of these stories would be likely to do. Each story is full of unusual happenings and is short enough for bed-time reading aloud – or later on for children to read to themselves.

ELIZABETH and DONALD ROSE, *The Big River*, Faber, London, 1963.

The story of a river from its source to where it joins the sea, told simply and illustrated with a marvellous feeling for water and watery creatures.

DIANA ROSS (illustrated by Leslie Wood), *The Story of the Little Red Engine*, Faber, London, 1969; Transatlantic Arts, Levittown.

A popular story of the little train journeying through the country, greeted by animals as he goes from station to station. There are accompanying noises for the listener to make during the reading.

JOHN RYAN (illustrated by the author) *Captain Pugwash*, Bodley Head, London, 1957; Picture Puffin, Harmondsworth, 1969.

Some pirates are not what they seem. Captain Pugwash brags and bullies (unless there is danger afoot) but he sees himself as handsome and brave. When Cut-throat Jake, his fiercest enemy, comes his way, he has to rely on Tom, the cabin boy of the *Black Pig* to save him. A story that is light-hearted and exciting.

CAROLYN SLOAN (illustrated by Fritz Wegner), *Carter is a Painter's Cat*, Kestrel (formerly Longman Young Books), Harmondsworth, 1971; Simon and Schuster, New York, 1971.

What happens when the not quite complete picture of Carter on the easel comes to life? And what happens when Carter himself takes up painting? A story told with sparkling wit, with illustrations that match the author's inventiveness on every page.

TOMI UNGERER (illustrated by the author), *Zeralda's Ogre*, Bodley Head, London, 1970; Picture Puffin, Harmondsworth, 1972; Harper-Row, New York, 1967.

A witty story of Zeralda the fearless girl whose ability to prepare the most delicious food dissuaded a very grouchy lot of ogres from eating children. Splendid illustrations.

MARJORIE-ANN WATTS, *Mulroy's Magic*, Faber, London, 1971; Young Puffin, Harmondsworth, 1975.

The grandfather clock stands in the bathroom. The bed is in the kitchen. If you interfere with these arrangements you will be turned into a goldfish – at least if your doll's house has been taken over by a tiny witch as Lucy's was in one of the stories in this book.

BRIAN WILDSMITH (illustrated by the author), *FABLES: The Lion and the Rat*; *The Hare and the Tortoise*; *The Miller, the Boy and the Donkey*; *The North Wind and the Sun*; *The Rich Man and the Shoemaker*; Oxford University Press, London.

A well-chosen selection of fables in which the moral of each is brought home by the text and by the cumulative power of the beautiful Wildsmith pictures.

URSULA MORAY WILLIAMS (illustrated by Peggy Fortnum), *Adventures of the Little Wooden Horse*, Young Puffin, Harmondsworth.

The little wooden horse sets off to sell himself in order to save his master. On the way he has some extraordinary adventures and shows how brave he is and how well his determination helps him through all misfortune until at last he returns home triumphant.

GENE ZION (illustrated by Margaret Bloy Graham), *Harry the Dirty Dog*, Bodley Head, London, 1960; Picture Puffin, Harmondsworth, 1970; Harper-Row, New York, 1956.

Harry, who hated being bathed, buries the scrubbing brush in the back garden and goes off to have a good dirty time. When he misses the family and feels hungry he runs all the way home but nobody recognizes him because he is so dirty. He tries his familiar tricks but he is not recognized until he is bathed and brushed.

9 Diane Discovers Letters

When Diane was nearly four years old she was painting 'an old lady with a big hat. She's sitting in the sun and she's feeling a bit sleepy. Now she's sleeping. You see I've made her eyes closed. She's snoring a little bit.' To which her mother replied: 'Yes, I can see she's having a lovely quiet sleep and her big hat will keep the sun out of her eyes.'

DIANE: 'Yes it will. It's her best hat for sleeping in.'

MOTHER: 'I'm glad she has such a nice hat because it makes her much more interesting.'

DIANE: 'It's my best picture. Will you put my name on it?'

MOTHER: 'Yes, of course. Where shall I write your name?'

DIANE: 'Draw it at the top.'

MOTHER: 'You help me.'

DIANE: 'Yes.'

MOTHER: 'What shall I begin with?'

DIANE: 'Draw some letters.'

MOTHER: 'I'll write the letters of your name with this paint brush, shall I?'

DIANE: 'Yes. Do the letters.'

MOTHER: 'What comes first?'

DIANE: 'I don't know.'

MOTHER: 'Dee comes first. Dee for Diane.'

DIANE: 'Dee for Diane. Yes, do dee.'

MOTHER: 'Watch. [*completes capital D*] That's dee for Diane.'

DIANE: 'Dee for Diane. That's my name [*pointing to the Capital D*].'

MOTHER: 'That's the first letter of your name. There are five letters in your name.'

DIANE: 'Five ...! One, two, three, four, five! Five letters in my name! Do them for me.'

MOTHER: 'Watch. First dee for Diane. Then ie with a dot, aye, en and then ee.'

DIANE: 'Now I'll do it. Let me do it.'

MOTHER: 'Have a new piece of paper.'

DIANE: 'I can do it. [*She writes with her paint brush, making a large shape something between D and O*]. I can write. Can't I? I can.'

On almost all the pictures following this one, Diane fixed a somewhat clumsy D shape. Then one day her mother said 'Shall I show you how to made D my way?' Diane did not appear to be very interested: 'I can do D for Diane.' Wisely, her mother did not insist on this. Soon Diane began to use her name as it appeared on her drinking mug as a model on which she based her writing. She was very interested in this from time to time, interpreting her task in a variety of ways. Sometimes she wrote one or two letters and then stopped. At other times she would begin with D or with E, proceeding either from left to right or (equally happily) from right to left. She liked letter i and made the dot very emphatically.

The letters she produced varied very much in size, some letters being very large and some quite small. Similarly the movements of her hand varied the positioning of the letters too. She often made letter E from the bottom to the top and put the horizontal line wherever she chose. Thus: ϲ ℓ ℮ ℺. Letter N was varied too: ∟ ∧ һ ⊓. Letter A gave her some trouble and was obviously written the wrong way round in some versions: Ᏸ ȼ ᶐ ᒋ ⍁. She often wrote D i n for Diane.

Her mother always accepted what she did with encouraging comments and without criticism. As a result Diane went on confidently. Sometimes she would make a few letter shapes on a piece of paper, fold it up and leave it for her father. On one occasion she said: 'I've written a big letter for you. It has dee for Diane and some other things as well.' Then she added: 'I can't write everything for you. Only some things.' Her father responded to this and with a bright orange pen he wrote 'Dear Diane, I like your letters. Love from Daddy.' This was very exciting. It was pinned up at the side of her bed and she had it read to her until she had memorized the text. She then 'read' it for herself. Sometimes she would invent other messages and 'read' these instead. She then made up letters of her own with invented letter shapes mixed up with those she already knew. When she was asked what her new letters 'said' she usually made up a lengthy reply.

This description of Diane's approach to reading and writing is given so as to establish what some children do and many more *could* do. It is not uncommon for the very young to be underestimated concerning their natural abilities and overestimated in what parents expect of them. If the achievements described above and the friendly, relaxed atmosphere within which they were made are examined carefully, it is clear that Diane is confident and eager to learn. She is assured of a share of adult company and adult awareness in all she is doing. She feels the security of her human environment. She is offered a wide range of uncomplicated materials and helped to enable her to exploit these. She is busy learning about the world around her. She is also busy finding out about herself and about her place in the world. No one dictates to her so frequently that this becomes a dominant feature of her upbringing. She elaborates on her experience in her own terms but in the company of people who offer her stable, affectionate responses. Alongside these they provide her with new experiences. Through their behaviour to one another she learns about the way they think and feel. She listens, watches and participates in day to day living without too much obvious restraint.

This, then, is the setting in which her learning takes place. We have considered a fragment relating to her discovery of reading and writing without relating this in turn to the wide range of other pursuits in which she is equally if not more involved. The place occupied by literacy is a small one and quite rightly so. Like all children she has a great need to develop all her interests with whatever priority she herself accords them. Parents can interfere too much in the way children select activities to fit their own interests, disposition and general needs. Far better to be happy-go-lucky than strained with anxiety and the desire to have a 'clever' child in the family.

It is very difficult for literate adults to understand what it is like to be illiterate, but it seems much easier for many people to make allowances for the very young than for older children. The most fortunate children begin while such learning is still part of their natural play. The unfortunate are those who receive enforced instruction or whose needs are almost totally ignored.

Using A B Cs

Diane's incidental writing and reading are activities she willingly undertakes, and the more so because she is able to share them with others. The talk that these provide and the pride of participation ('I can do it. I can'), are important because they establish ways of thinking, observing and doing. It would, however, be foolish to pretend that she has, at the stage we left her, enough information to proceed very far. She is soon going to need more help.

Already she delights in hearing stories and rhymes. She remembers many of these in detail. It is to these that she now returns with renewed interest, having made the discovery that the marks on the paper, the letters, words and sentences, carry the language of the stories she listens to. She is beginning to formulate the questions: How do you do it ? How do you read all these letters ? How did they get written in the first place ? Can I do it too ? The answers to most children should be first: 'I'll show you' and 'Yes, of course you can do it.' (Children who have special disabilities may need specialist help at the appropriate time. They should not be thought less well of because they will take longer and they should have a full share of talk and of story-reading until they are ready for participating in reading and writing).

Of course not all books for children are story books or books of verse. There are other kinds of books to enjoy, books that give general information and help children to understand what numbers stand for. Indeed there may be times when books like Richard Scarry's will be constant companions. Among such 'teaching' books are some of the many A B Cs which are now available (see pp. 106–8). It is in these that children can find some of the new information they need in order to understand what letters are.

Four kinds of information are to be found in A B Cs:

(1) Information about the visual appearance of letters: their shapes. This information is usually given about small (lower-case) letters and capital (upper-case) letters.
(2) Information about the linguistic meaning of the letters: what each letter stands for. This information is always selective and therefore incomplete. It is of the nature of A B Cs that they present this

information by drawing attention to the first letter of each printed word and thus to the first sound of the spoken version of the printed word. (This obviously cannot work for letter x which is found at the end of written words (e.g. fox, box). When used at the beginning of certain works of Greek origin like xylophone, letter x stands for the zed sound.)

(3) General information which comes from the animals, objects, people, etc., chosen to illustrate the linguistic meaning of the letters. This may be organized round set subjects such as zoo animals, baby animals, toys, familiar objects or on a more general formula. They may also employ one example for each letter or a number of examples. Some may also have a continuous text.

(4) Information about the alphabetical order of letters. Letters have to be presented in some order. The traditional order is of very little significance to children; they cannot use this information for any task other than learning the alphabet off by heart. There is no harm in this so long as it is not thought that this constitutes 'knowing the alphabet'. There is much more than this to 'knowing' the letters.

One of the chief omissions from ABCs is the set of consonant symbols made up of two letters, the second of which is letter h: ch, sh, th, wh and the less common ph. These are sometimes used in the examples given but included under c, s, t, w, or p. Thus *ship* may appear under s and *church* under c. This follows dictionary practice but ABCs are not dictionaries, rather collections of letters and words to illustrate the way initial letters in printed words correspond to initial sounds in these words as they appear in spoken form. There is a good reason for including the two-letter symbols (digraphs): children need this information as much as any of the other information an ABC supplies and much more than 'X stands for xylophone.'

An ABC is a summary – and frequently a very good one – of the two sets of letter shapes, upper- and lower-case letters and a selection of words which are usually (but not always) nouns. These are illustrated to provide a context for the words and it is the picture rather than the word which will initiate response from the child. No ABC is much good on its own – except as a picture book. Help from an adult – or another child – will be necessary to make the connections between object depicted (e.g. elephant), letter shapes (E e) and the sound at the beginning of the word. Further help is also needed if the child is to explore the visual qualities which the letters have and the differences that exist between one letter and all the others.

Diane began with her own name and incorporated in this one example were bits of valuable information, which, when repeated several times, became important clues to the nature of written English:

(1) D is for Diane. (This suggests that D is special to the word Diane but she may not know in what way this is so, or how this is shared by many other words, until many other examples are used: e.g. D is also for dog, doll, daddy.)
(2) D is the first letter of the word. (Positioning of letters in word. The first letter in English words is the first on the left.)
(3) Diane has five letters. (Number of letters in word.)
(4) This one is D, and so on. (Pointing to letters as objects and giving names.)
(5) This is the shape of D. (Demonstrating handwriting movements and drawing attention to the shape of the letter.)
(6) This is your name. (The shape of the whole word.)
(7) I'll write Diane for you. (Direction of writing – left to right; spaces between letters and the positioning of letters on an invisible writing line.)

When Diane was shown how her name was written, she needed to do it for herself. She then practised in a variety of contexts and finally used her knowledge and skill to 'write a letter' to her father. She thus demonstrated an understanding that the word *letter* has two meanings. The letter was the paper she folded up. The paper had on it a large letter D. As soon as she received a letter in return for hers, she needed to know 'what it said'. She had begun to look consciously at words and ask questions about reading and writing. She quickly memorized the text of the letter and then made up imaginary letters. She was not yet conscious in any precise way of what each word was but considered the message as a whole. Next she invented letter shapes and produced pages on which there were many marks, some of which were Ds. She then began to copy her father's letter in bed and gave him this. During this activity she suddenly discovered that Daddy had a D just as Diane had. This was very satisfying. It was not until some time later that the D page of an A B C made her realize that many words began with D and the search for these was on. To begin with she made as many wrong suggestions as right suggestions for words beginning with the sound dee and this initiated a new move in the game: If it's not D *what is it ?* What are the possibilities ? The A B C then became more than just a book to look at. It became a source of specific information which she was beginning to understand.

A B C Books

ANONYMOUS, *Peter Piper's Practical Principles of Plain and Perfect Pronunciation*, Dover, New York, 1970.

Facsimile of the 1830 edition, in which the tongue-twister is exploited in teaching children about letters and sounds. This is the little book in which 'Peter Piper picked a peck of pickled peppers' first appeared. Each tongue-twister is accompanied by a quaint wood-cut in black and white.

ANGELA BANNER (illustrated by Bryan Ward), *Ant and Bee; An Alphabetical Story for Tiny Tots*, Kaye and Ward, London, 1951; Watts, New York, 1958.

A story that links the letter of the alphabet in a somewhat contrived manner. 'Ant lived with a great friend of his, who was a Bee. Ant and Bee lived in a Cup.' Despite the unlikeliness of it all, some children enjoy hearing this book again and again.

DICK BRUNA, *B is for Bear*, Methuen, London, 1971.

On each page the child's attention is drawn to the object which illustrates the way letters correspond to sounds. An appropriate context is created for each object and by means of special colour, the child is helped to identify this without confusion. The illustrations are in the 'chunky' style of this author-artist's extensive list of books.

JOHN BURNINGHAM, *A. B. C.*, Jonathan Cape, London, 1964; Bobbs, Indianapolis, 1967.

A book with touches of humour in the way this fine artist uses colour to depict the objects he presents.

CHARLOTTE HOUGH, *My Aunt's Alphabet*, Hamish Hamilton, London, 1969.

An ABC with a running text in which appropriate words are picked out of the solid colour on which they are printed and surrounded by white. This makes it possible to draw attention to adjectives, verbs and conjunctions, as well as nouns. Thus the pages for B read: 'When I did my sums *Billy* hit me with my *big bat*. *Bonk*. My aunt sent him to *bed but* he *bit* her. He can *be* a *bad baby*.' The book ends with an index in which all the words in the text are arranged alphabetically.

HELEN OXENBURY, *A. B. C. of Things*, Heinemann, London, 1971; Watts, New York, 1972.

A number of 'things' illustrated with gentle humour by a fine, original artist.

RODNEY PEPPÉ, *The Alphabet Book*, Kestrel (formerly Longman Young Books), Harmondsworth, 1968; Scholastic Books Services, New York, 1968.

Stylish pictures of objects which are linked together by means of a simple text: 'This is the *a*nchor that holds the *b*oat.'

CELESTINO PIATTI, *Animal A. B. C.*, Benn, London, 1965; Atheneum, New York, 1966.

A distinguished artist whose work is certainly very satisfying for adults. Its resonance brings to mind stained glass. And the colours used have a depth and power which is matched by highly skilled but simple drawing.

MAURICE SENDAK, *Alligators All Round*, Collins, London, 1968; Harper & Row, New York, 1962.

Here you will find alligators catching cold, getting giggles, making macaroni and riding reindeer and a touch of madness that will help to bring home the points ABCs try to make.

Also by MAURICE SENDAK in the same series, the *Nutshell Library*, in which each book has pages only four inches by three inches: *One Was Johnny*, Collins, London, 1968; Harper & Row, New York 1962.

An original counting book in the style of 'this is the house that Jack built'.

BRIAN WILDSMITH, *Brian Wildsmith's ABC*, Watts, New York, 1963.

A book of great distinction. Paintings of objects and animals in brilliant colours with labels in lower-case and upper-case letters.

Counting Books

Counting books do not teach children to count any more or less than ABCs teach them to read. Nevertheless, they are useful in establishing links between numbers of objects and numerals. They also help children to read numerals. It is sometimes overlooked that these are very different from words in that each *stands for a word*, very much as Chinese characters do. Thus the figure 3 stands for both a certain number of objects as well as the word three (if one is English) or the word trois (if one is French). Numerals are international unlike the words associated with them.

ERIC CARLE, *One, Two, Three, to the Zoo*, Hamish Hamilton, London, 1969.

On every double page a numeral is matched by the corresponding number of animals travelling by train. The pictures do much more than support mathematical ideas: a careful look at them will reveal details out of which several stories can be made up.

SUSANNA GRETZ, *Teddy Bears One to Ten*, Benn, London, 1969; Follett, Chicago, 1968.

You have probably never seen quite so many 'character' teddy bears ever before. They add up to a witty, slightly wicked lot who look as if they will be up to no good as soon as tea is over.

DEAN HAY, *Now I Can Count*, Collins, London, 1968; Lion Press New York, 1968.

A first counting book of colour photographs numbering up to twelve. Also a series of photographs illustrating the times of the day.

TANA HOBAN (photographed by the author), *Count and See*, Macmillan, London, 1972.

Each left-hand page has a numeral and a matching pattern of dots; on the right-hand page a black-and-white photograph illustrates the relevant number – in dustbins, eggs, pigeons and so on. The pictures are satisfying without counting, so the very young can also share this book.

JOHN LANGSTAFF (illustrated by Feodor Rojanovsky), *Over in the Meadow*, Harcourt Brace Johanovich, New York, 1973.

A rhyming (not to say singing) counting book with animals and their young nicely illustrated. The music has been added to the last page.

RODNEY PEPPÉ, *Circus Numbers*, Kestrel (formerly Longman Young Books), Harmondsworth, 1969; Delacorte, New York, 1969.

Another circus book with fine clear pictures to accompany the ring master, the horses, acrobats, elephants (a hundred) etc. At the top of each page there are blue stars to help with the counting of the objects in the pictures.

YUTAKA SUGITA, *One to Eleven*, Evans Brothers, London, 1971.

Wistful pictures of a child who encounters one owl, two giraffes (who lend their necks to make a swing), three flowers (blooming from the mouth of a trumpet) and so on, with a surprise on almost every page.

10   The Letter-Shapes Game

Diane's first awareness of letters came when she first had her name attached to a picture of an old lady sleeping. At this time she was nearly four years old. Her interest in letters, in letter shapes and in writing fluctuated according to what new learning she was undertaking. Thus her interest in sentences, in word matching and word recognition displaced an interest in letters for periods of time in which she was acquiring a new understanding of these aspects of reading and writing. Letters and the sounds they represent were of interest to her at precisely the moments when her need for this kind of information increased her understanding of all the processes she was mastering. So when she was between four and five years old she showed sporadic involvement with letters and sounds; this is where she started but not where she stayed consistently. The letter-shapes game, and the picture- and word-matching game became more important to Diane as she fitted the skills of reading and writing into a more and more coherent pattern. When she was around six years old she took up the study of letters with much more detailed interest than she had shown previously, influenced this time by what was going on at school.

One day Diane took some sheets on which she had previously painted her name. With round-nosed scissors she cut out each letter and looked at them with great pleasure. They were not well cut out but they were freed from the paper and could be manipulated. As a result of this interest her mother made another set with card from a cereal carton. She showed them to Diane who began without delay to place them in the order in which they occurred in her name. She made some mistakes but corrected these by comparing what she had done by matching each letter against those on her drinking mug. When she no longer found this interesting, she began looking at the letters separately. She then found a page in one of her ABCs for each of the five letters.

These discoveries which originated in very homely, informal learning situations with little attempt at formal instruction on anyone's part were the beginning of Diane's study of letters. It is an interesting example of how children can reach an understanding of abstract problems without being 'pushed' into it. By the time Diane began to try writing words for herself, she had played with bricks with painted letters. These, however, did not interest her much. Then she was given a set of magnetic letters and sometimes she would use these to make words on the refrigerator door. But it was the accident of cutting out large letters that gave her most satisfaction and stimulated her curiosity about the nature of letters.

Long before she knew much about letter names and the sounds represented by letters (letter values), she had discovered that she had to know which way up the letters go. One day she wrote bu*ƨ* on one of her pages. At this time she had done little handwriting other than her name. Everyone in the family showed their pleasure in this and the picture on which her writing appeared was stuck on the fridge door. Only her brother commented on the way she had reversed the letter S. She was puzzled by this and to help her her mother made a large letter S and cut it out. Together, she and Diane looked at how the letter could be placed on paper.

DIANE: 'You see, it can go like this (S) or like that (ƨ). I did it like that didn't I?'

MOTHER: 'Yes, but you didn't know about it did you?'

DIANE: 'I didn't know it had two ways it can go.'

MOTHER: 'Well, it has two ways it *can* go but we only use one way. We don't need two ways do we?'

DIANE: 'No we don't. But it can go two ways can't it?'

MOTHER: 'Yes it can but you have to learn which way we use, otherwise people will not be able to read what you write will they? Get one of your ABCs and we'll have a look at it.'

[*Diane fetched one and the page with S was found.*]

MOTHER: 'You see. Here it is. Which way does it go?'

[Diane took the cut-out letter and put it on the page thus (ƨ).]

DIANE: 'No that's the other way isn't it. Like in my picture. So it has to go like this (S).'

MOTHER: 'That's right. Now you know about S.'

DIANE: 'But I might forget.'

MOTHER: 'Well that won't matter. When you've done it a lot of times you'll remember, I'm sure.'

When her father came home he was told all about this latest discovery and after Diane was in bed, her mother suggested that he make a game for Diane. He took some card from cartons in Diane's junk box and made large, easy-to-handle letters in clear script with a thick black felt pen. Then at his wife's suggestion, he made a matching 'board' on which he reproduced all the letter shapes, so that Diane could match the cut-out letters to those on the board. As there was no card large enough for this he used part of a large brown shopping bag. When he began to think about the order to show letter-shapes on the matching board, his first thought was to place them in alphabetic order. He quickly abandoned this idea because it had nothing to do with letter-shapes. After some time his planning produced no satisfactory ordering of the letters so he decided to consult a teacher friend about the matter. They finally decided to place letter-shapes together in such a way that similar letter-shapes and letter-shapes with features that were easily confused could be compared and talked about, as shown on page 113 and as follows:

First line: **o, c, a, l. o** is presented as a basic shape, with **c** and **a** derived from it. The addition of **l** prepares for the way **o** + **l** become **d, b, p**, and **g**.

Second line: **g, e, d, b. g** is placed immediately below **o** to show

---

LAY-OUT OF MATCHING BOARD

The board should be large enough for all the letter shapes to be laid out on it. If card from a box is used, it can be hinged with sellotape so that it folds into a convenient form for storage. Make sure that the fold does not pass through any letter shape. The board can also be made of thick paper (such as paper from old carrier-bags). It can then be rolled up when not in use.

LETTER SHAPES

The letter shapes may be traced on to card (blank postcards will do) and then drawn with a black marker pen. It is important to make them carefully and to avoid any variation to the shapes which come from adult handwriting. They should not be made *smaller* than is shown here. Children must learn to recognize the basic elements which make up the shape of each letter. Handwritten letters are often modified in ways which are unhelpful to children.

Board for letter-matching

o	c	a	l
g	e	d	b
t	f	b	p
n	h	n	m
i	j	u	r
s	z	v	w
k	x	y	q

Board for letter-matching

o a

c e

d b

l i k f

j t n

m r s

v y w

p q g

x z u h

how the addition of the **l** shape and the hook make the new letter. **e** is related to the **c** above and **d** and **a**. The **b** is placed back to back with **d** and relates to the **l** shape above it.

Third line: **t, f, b, p**. **t** and **f** are placed together to show how alike they are in their basic shape. The shape of either has only to be turned up and over to make the other. Letter shape **b** is placed under **d** in the second line to allow the two to be compared from another position. Letter shape **p** is then found to be next to **b** in both lines and its similarity may be seen by showing how the **o** shape is attached to the **l** shape.

Fourth line: **n, h, n, m**. Here the basic shape **n** is found in **h** and **m**. The differences, an **l** shape in the **h** and a double **n** shape in the **m** are easy to distinguish. (Diane's father made **m** equal to two **n**'s placed side by side.)

Fifth line: **i, j, u, r**. Letters **i** and **j** are placed together because of the dot each has. **u** is placed under **n** in the fourth line, and **r** is related to the **m** shape, **r** being an incompleted **n**.

Sixth line: **s, z, v, w**. (When Diane first looked at the matching board, she said 'Where's ess?' And as this was the letter-shape that began the business of the new game, she expected to see it first. Her father said: 'I've hidden it among all the letters to see if you can find it.' Diane didn't find it for some time because she was temporarily confused by the sight of so many letters. 'There's such a lot of letters,' she said. 'Oh, not *so* many. Look carefully along all the lines of letters.' Her father handed her the **s** shape he had cut out and helped her to check each until she found it.) Letter **s** starts in an anti-clockwise direction, reverses half way and finishes in a clockwise direction. Letter **z** is the reverse of this – at least it would be so, if it were a curved letter. Both **s** and **z** are letter shapes children tend to write the wrong way round. Here they can talk about the differences and by manipulating the letters, 'see' these differences. Letters **v** and **w** are related shapes – **w** being two **v**'s stuck together.

Seventh line: **k, x, y, q**. This line was used for the letters that were felt to be of least importance. **y** was placed below **v** to show how the two shapes are related, **y** having the right hand side of the **v** extended downwards. Letter **q** was left in the corner opposite **k**, because it is associated with the same sound as **k**.

When the letter shapes had been cut out, including two **b**'s and two **n**'s (in all, twenty-eight letter-shapes), Diane's father placed them on the shopping bag paper and marked round them lightly with a pencil. He then chose the brightest colours from Diane's coloured pens and linked letters by colour. He was careful to leave plenty of space round each letter-shape. The cut-out letter-shapes were stored in a big envelope.

Diane's reaction to the game was mixed. At first she played it cheerfully with whoever would spare time but after a time she put it away. Her father thought he had probably made a mistake in pressing this on her. Later, however, he was proved wrong. Diane returned to the letter-shapes game from time to time, usually when she had received from some source, a new awareness of one of the letters. The game provided for much talk about letter shapes, as we show here:

o (oh)*: circle, round, ball.

c (cee): not quite a whole circle; a bit is missing on one side; on the right there's a gap in the circle.

a (ay): like **c** too but with a little straight line down one side, the right side.

l (ell): an easy one: a straight line – it's as long as the line in **d**, **p** and **b**.

g (gee): like **c** but with a straight line down one side; the right side; the line has a curve at the bottom like a tail.

e (ee): like **c** but with a little straight line across. It shuts off the top bit.

d (dee): another one like **a** and like **p**, but it has a longer straight line than **a** – on the same side as **a**, the right side.

b (bee): another one like **a** the other way round; a long straight line – just the opposite of **d**.

t (tee): this one has a straight line and a tail on one side – the right side; it has a little line across the straight line near the top.

f (eff): like **t** turned upside down – a curve at the top coming from the right, then a straight line going down; a little line going across, just below the curve.

p (pee): one like **a** the other way round but a long side going down on one side, the left side.

***

*The traditional names are seldom written and will look odd at first sight.

n (en): this one's new. It has a shape like a tunnel or like a bridge with a hump. It's like two short straight lines joined at the top by a curve.

h (aitch): this one's like **n**. The longer straight line is on the left, it goes up above the **n** bit. This is what makes it different from **n**.

m (em): this one's like two **n**'s stuck together; two tunnels side by side; two bridges with humps.

i (ie): a little straight line with a dot just above it. So **j** and **i** both have dots, **i** has no tail.

j (jay): a bit like **f** turned over and around; it has a straight line and a tail turned to the left, but it also has a dot above it.

u (yew): this is just like **n** upside down, and then turned from left to right.

r (arr): this one's like an **n** that wasn't finished on one side – the right side. The right side is missing. It's got a little straight line with a curve on top. The curve goes to the right.

s (ess): this one's got twisted like a snake. It starts like **c** and then it changes and twists round the other way – like having an upside down **c** stuck on to the first one ᶜ∍. They join together in the middle.

z (zed or zee): this one is a zig-zag. It has a little line at the top and a little line at the bottom. They're joined together with a straight line that slants. The slanting line goes from the right side on the top to the left side of the bottom.

v (vee): two little lines like the top bit of **X**:**X**. The lines come together at the bottom: two fingers can make a **v**. It's like a roof upside down.

w (double-yew): like two **v**'s stuck together.

k (kay): it starts like **l**, then it has two little lines coming out from its middle: one goes slanting up, the other comes slanting down.

x (ex): a criss-cross; two little lines criss cross; like a kiss at the bottom of a letter.

y (wye): slanting lines again; one little one and one long one; the long one is on the right side. It's like **x** with one bit missing **x**.

q (kew): one that is like **g** and like **a**; but it can have a long line going down on one side: the right, and it can have a little tail going the opposite way to **g**.

These are examples of the kind of talking that will help children to notice the shapes of letters. They will be helped to memorize the shapes by putting the shaping process into words.

The names of letters may be learned bit by bit. At this stage, it is shapes that are important not the names: being able to say a, b, c, etc. doesn't mean children can recognize the letters. Names are labels for making it easy to refer to each letter-shape. In many cases, the name of a letter gives a clue to a sound associated with that letter. The names of the letters and what the shapes mean is dealt with in the Picture and Word-Matching Game described in Chapter 12.

As well as matching the shapes, children may like, as Diane did, to make the shapes for themselves. Many ingenious ways of making drawn shapes, before letters appear and afterwards, will be discovered by children – making shapes on dusty surfaces or in sand with a finger or a stick. They may also like to make shapes in a pat of clay or dough, or to use large paint brushes to paint shapes on to newspaper. Finger painting can also be used for writing. The 'feel' of the finger on paper is a help to some children. Jam is lovely for this and chocolate can be a delight – to the child shape-maker.

All sorts of scrap materials can also be used for making letter shapes, with glue or paste to stick them to any available paper. Straight line letters like l, k, x, y, v, w, i, may be made with used whole match-sticks and halved sticks. Strips of thin card or scraps of material can be stuck on to paper. Round shapes can be cut out of card or scraps of material and combined with match sticks or straight pieces of the right length to make letters like o, c, e, a. The group made from a – that is d, b, p, g, q – can be made together so that their origin in one shape (and hence their similarity) can be talked about. Their difference depends very much on how they are *turned in space*. Try making one shape – say shape d – turn d over to the right and it becomes b.

RULES OF THE GAME

Lastly, there are four essential rules for adults in playing this game:

(1) Never let the game become boring. If a child's matching of the letter-shapes is random this is a sure sign that the game ought not to be played.

(2) Don't use it if it is not a success. Stop playing when interest sags.

(3) Allow the child to return to it whenever he wants to.

(4) Let the child dispense with it whether it has been exhausted as a game or not.

Many children like to put things on one side for a time and then return to them later when they may well have thought about them a good deal. They will only want to use any aid when it offers them the help they need. They will cease to use any aid which is no longer of any use to them.

The right moment for this game is difficult to predict. What is well-suited to some children at three years of age is not so for many children until they are five or six. Nothing is ever gained by confronting children with educational activities, however worthy they may be, if they are not immediately successful and totally enjoyable. Children learn readily only if they are secure and confident and, above all, if they are interested in what they are doing. This applies equally to playing with water, listening to stories, building with chairs and cushions, asking questions and listening to the answers, or writing like Diane and Patrick.

11   The Sentence-Making Game

Diane discovered the Sentence-Making Game for herself when she was nearly five. It was the result of an accident when she was trimming the pages of a book she was making. The scissors accidentally cut off one of the words her father had written underneath a picture of giraffes in the zoo. Diane had asked for the words 'A man and lady giraffe in the zoo.' It was the word zoo that became detached. At first she did not notice anything but then she found the word among the pieces of paper she had trimmed. She then went to her mother.

DIANE: 'Look what I've done. I've cut some writing off one of the pages.'

MOTHER: 'So you have. Can you find where it should go?'

DIANE: 'I don't know 'cos I've just found it.'

MOTHER: 'Maybe we can stick it back on if you can find where it goes. Why don't you have a look?'

DIANE: [*looking at it carefully*] 'What is it?'

MOTHER: 'Don't you remember about the giraffes?'

DIANE: 'Yes, I do. Does it go there?'

MOTHER: 'Well, go and see if it does.'

[*Diane found the page and looked at the writing.*]

DIANE: 'I remember. It's a lady and a man giraffe picture isn't it?'

MOTHER: 'Yes it is. Where were they?'

DIANE: 'At the zoo.'

MOTHER: 'So let's read what you asked daddy to write for you. What's this word?' [*pointing to man.*]

DIANE: 'It has M. Oh, yes! I remember, it's man! It's man!'

MOTHER: 'So now remember what Daddy wrote for you.'

DIANE: 'A man giraffe and a lady giraffe.'

MOTHER: 'Well done. And where are they in the picture?'

DIANE: 'In the zoo.'

MOTHER: 'Yes. So now read it with me.'

DIANE: ' A man giraffe . . .'

MOTHER: 'Wait a moment, look at all the words. Where's "giraffe"?'

DIANE: 'Here.' [*pointing to giraffe*]

MOTHER: 'Yes. You remembered. So, how many words like giraffe are in Daddy's writing? Let's look.'

DIANE: 'There's only this one. But there are two giraffes.'

MOTHER: 'And what did you say to Daddy?'

DIANE: 'I said they were a man and a lady giraffe.'

MOTHER: 'So that makes two doesn't it?'

DIANE: 'One man giraffe and one lady giraffe.'

MOTHER: 'So, let's read it.'

DIANE: 'A man and a lady giraffe.'

MOTHER: [*having pointed to the words as they were read*] 'And what about this?' [*indicating 'in'*].

DIANE: [*with triumph*] 'In the zoo!'

MOTHER: 'Yes but look what you did. You cut off one word. Which one?'

DIANE: 'Zoo. I cut off zoo.'

MOTHER: 'And it sounds funny without zoo: A man and the lady giraffe in the.'

DIANE: [*holding up the word*] 'Zoo!'

MOTHER: 'Zoo! That's right. But where can we put it now? There's no room.'

DIANE: 'Well, we can put it up at the top.'

MOTHER: 'But then it won't be with the rest of the writing. And every time we read it we'll say: A man and a lady giraffe in the.'

DIANE: 'Well I can put all the writing at the top.'

MOTHER: 'Yes you can do that. Can you do it yourself?'

DIANE: 'Yes. I can do it.'

On her own, Diane chose, as an adult might not have done, to cut out each word separately, helped in this task by the clear word spaces her father had incorporated in his handwriting.

DIANE: 'I've cut it all out. I'll get some sticky to put it at the top.'

MOTHER: 'Can you do it by yourself?'

DIANE: 'Yes, but what comes first?'

MOTHER: [*coming to look at what Diane has done*] 'Oh, I see.

That's what you've done. You've made the writing into separate words.'

DIANE: 'Yes, I have.'

MOTHER: 'So now you have put them together again.'

DIANE: 'I know. But you help me.'

MOTHER: 'You know what I'll do?'

DIANE: 'What?'

MOTHER: 'I'll write it for you again and then you'll see how the words go.'

[*Mother then wrote 'a man and a lady giraffe in the zoo' in handwriting the same size as the original and placed it above the page in Diane's book.*]

MOTHER: 'Now you can see how they go. Put all the words the right way up.'

[*Diane did this by the side of her book.*]

DIANE: 'This one's first.' [*placing 'a' under her mother's handwriting*].

MOTHER: 'And then?'

DIANE: '"man". This is "man". Now this one. What's this one?'

MOTHER: '"and".'

DIANE; 'Oh yes "and a lady".' [*Repeats*] '"a man and a lady giraffe"'! That goes next. Now there's only three left.'

MOTHER: 'You can do them can't you?'

DIANE: 'This one [*taking up "in"*]. '"in the zoo" has to be next hasn't it?'

MOTHER: 'Yes, "in" goes next. [*observing*] Good, what word is that?'

DIANE: 'It's one I know.'

MOTHER: [*repeats, and as she does, points to each word*] '"in", "the", "zoo". So what's this one?' [*pointing to "the"*].

DIANE: 'It's "the".'

MOTHER: ' – and this one?'

DIANE: 'Zoo! That's the one I cut off by mistake isn't it? Because it comes at the end.'

MOTHER: 'That's right. So now put a little blob of sticky on each word and stick them down.'

Diane proceeds to do so on her own. When she is finished, she takes her mother's handwritten version and once more cuts the text into separate words. When her mother comes to see how she is getting on, Diane is matching the words and repeating them. When she has finished she is very pleased with her achievement, and says, 'I want to keep my words.'

She found a used envelope and stored her words in this. A few days later she matched the words against the writing she had stuck together and asked for the writing that was to go on the next page to be done in the same way.

When she had decided what she wished to have written for her, this was produced twice; once for cutting out and the other for matching. And again, when this part of the game was complete, she cut the version that remained into words and stored them in her envelope. By the time the book she was making was complete she had the words for the following sentences:

(1) a man and a lady giraffe in the zoo.
(2) the lion is sleeping.
(3) a man gives the penguins fish to eat.

Now when all the words had been taken out of the envelope, the matching game was much harder and Diane's interest was caught by the way in which words from her collection could be combined in new ways. The random order in which they were taken from the envelope sometimes produced a new piece of writing and Diane's discovery of this led her to exclaim: 'I can make writing myself!' She ran to fetch someone to see what she had done and her brother came to look. He too was intrigued by the possibilities of this game. Her father too joined in.

FATHER: 'Good, Diane, read it to me?'

DIANE: 'It's my writing.'

FATHER: 'Yes but I can read it too. You can't read it can you?'

DIANE: 'Yes I can' [*reads, pointing to each word*] 'penguins sleeping in the zoo.'

FATHER: 'What else can you make?' [*He helps to sort out all the words*].

DIANE: 'Three "a"s and three "the"s.' One "giraffe", one "lion", one "penguin", one "fish". . .'

BROTHER: 'That's not "penguin". It's "penguins" [*emphasizing the final s*].

DIANE: 'But if I cut it off it'll be "penguin", won't it?'

BROTHER: 'Look what I've made.'

DIANE [*reads slowly*]: '"the lady is sleeping in the zoo." That's not right. Ladies don't sleep in the zoo. I want to say: "the lady is eating fish and chips".'

DIANE (*beginning*): '"the lady is eat fish and . . ."'

FATHER: 'I think you need "ing" here' [*pointing to eat*]. 'For the lady is eating isn't she? You may cut it off from sleeping.'

[*Diane's brother does so.*]

DIANE [*to her brother*]: 'You've spoilt "sleeping" now'.

FATHER: 'No he hasn't. You can put the "ing" back whenever you like.' [*He shows Diane how to do this.*] 'See? You can make eating now and you can make fishing if you like.'

DIANE: 'I need "eating" don't I. Put it with eat.'

[*She puts it at the beginning. The new words reads* ingeat.]

BROTHER: 'Hey! not at the beginning, silly. Look.' [*He makes* eating *correctly.*]

DIANE: 'I knew that.'

BROTHER: 'If you knew why didn't you do it? You didn't know it!'

DIANE: 'Yes I did but I forgot.' [*She reads*] '"the lady is eating fish and"; I haven't got "chips".'

FATHER: 'I'll do it for you.' [*He writes* chips *on a new piece of paper*.]

DIANE: 'That's not very nice writing. But it will do.'

[*She adds* chips *to her writing and reads.*] '"Chips".'

She then fetched her mother to show her the results of the new game and for the next few days she spent some time drawing, asking for words to be written on the drawings and reconstructing the writing in this latest book by using the words stored in her envelope.

And so she discovered that any new piece of writing she wanted could, with a little help, be put together by manipulating her stored words. When new words were needed, these were written out on pieces of paper. Eventually the game became difficult, because of the number of words she had to store in one envelope. Her father then suggested that she should have one envelope for each page in her book and he prepared extra strips of paper for this purpose.

Sometimes she matched single words rather than whole sentences as, for instance, with another giraffe page on which the labels 'neck', 'legs', 'tail', 'mouth' appeared. Sometimes she matched the writing which she had dictated. It was not long before she herself wrote the new words she needed and like Patrick she based her spellings on what she knew about the sounds which the letters represent. Her brother sometimes pointed out mistakes she had made. She would then write out a new word card but he never commented on her rather slow and clumsy handwriting; she accepted his occasional help. As no one else remarked about her spelling when it did not represent words conventionally, she was never given cause to become anxious and afraid of this. She did everything with confidence and obvious enjoyment.

At this time her involvement with home-made books meant spending some time almost every day in using her new-found skills. Some of this time she spent on her own but though she did not ask for undivided attention from her mother and father she nevertheless felt the need to have someone there to talk to and seek help from as she worked. Sometimes someone sat down with her but when this was not possible, she did as much as she could by herself, talking about it all the time and happy to have responses from other members of the family, however busy they were. When nobody was available, she played on her own, often going back to consider what she had done earlier.

On no occasion did Diane ever show any desire to copy from books. It is important to note that all her word-matching and sentence-making began with interests of her own and were written down from her dictation. The skills she was practising made use of *her own ideas* expressed in *her own way*. She was thus saved from spending her time with what did not interest her or which she did not understand. The language of books and rhymes and the complex ideas these contain, influenced her thinking and her spoken language. From each repeated reading and re-telling of a story she learned to extract new meaning and to absorb the language of story-telling. It was some time before other writers started to have an influence on her writing. All through this early stage she was preoccupied with her own language.

To make the sentence-making game, little more than scrap materials, a black fibre-tipped pen and a pair of round-nosed scissors are needed. It is best if word and word endings (for instance 'ing', 'ed', 's') are all made the same size. A small block of thick, lined note-paper may be used or a pack of blank white post cards. Cards may be cut in half and all writing is printed in clear *lower-case* script centrally on each strip. The size of letters used should be similar to those on p. 114. Words should be cut out and new blank cards kept in an envelope with pen and scissors. Card stands up to handling better than paper and is preferable for this reason.

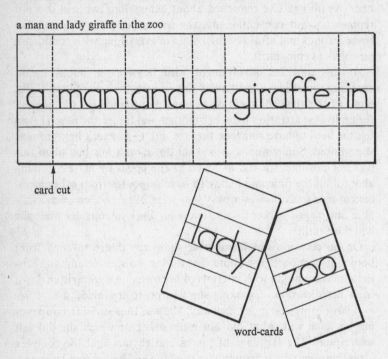

a man and lady giraffe in the zoo

card cut

word-cards

Great care should be taken to ensure that the handwriting is carefully done and that it does not include careless adult letter shapes. A tale out of school illustrates the important point that the letter shapes which children use in their early experience of reading and writing should contain as little variation as possible.

Jenny was a very careful child. She read well for her age and she had begun to write stories. One day a visitor came to the classroom and Jenny offered to read to her from a book in which the teacher had written sentences that she had previously made from printed and handwritten cards. The visitor was puzzled because she paused at the word **boy**. 'Is it a word?' asked the visitor. 'No, I don't think so. I don't think it is a word,' replied Jenny. The visitor then printed the word **boy** and asked the same question. This time the answer was immediate. 'Oh yes, that's the word boy.' The visitor was puzzled. 'Why is this not a word then?' she asked, pointing to the handwritten word **boy**. 'Well you see,' said Jenny, 'this one's got this rounded bit and this one hasn't.' After comparing **y** and **y** she discarded **y**; to her it looked quite different from **y**, and seemed to be a different letter.

As Diane's parents realized when they discussed the making of the letter-shapes game, some of our letters are differentiated by very small differences in shape. For instance, **h** and **n** differ only in the height of the ascender in **h**. (See also pages 112–21.) So make consistent use of one set of letter-shapes and do not introduce variations. Do not use capital letters because they are of little use and simply complicate the problem of letter recognition. The exceptions to this are proper names which may or may not be written with capital letters at the beginning of the name (a clear exception to the rule will be the word '**I**' which is always written as a capital letter. To write it as '**i**' would be confusing.

12   The Picture- and Word-Matching Game

It is sometimes said of children that they do not 'know their sounds'. How then would they talk if they did not, in some sense of the word, 'know' their sounds? They produce millions of them, like the rest of us, all day long. What exactly is it that they, the illiterates or beginners in literacy learning, do not 'know?'

(1) They do not have an awareness of sounds in isolation. They have no need for such information in order to become successful speakers. They are able to make speech-sounds but they do not know what each speech-sound is. Nor do they know 'how' they make their speech-sounds. As has already been said, only people who have some training in phonetics 'know their sounds' in this sense.

(2) They do not know how speech sounds and letters are associated. Letters, as visual marks, are silent. They do not 'say' anything. They represent something or other. The child needs to know what this something is. We give him ideas about this and many examples.

Thus, 'knowing their sounds' means becoming aware of speech sounds as little bits of language as well as 'knowing' the ways in which firstly, speech sounds stand for letters, and secondly, letters stand for speech sounds. The picture- and word-matching game proposed below provides some clues about matching sounds to letters and letters to sounds. In each case, a picture intervenes between sound and letter. The picture depicts an object. The child must be able to identify the object. The word standing for the object is spoken. Spoken word and written word are compared. The initial part of the spoken word and of the written word are given special attention. A sound is associated with a letter. A sound is said to be represented by a letter. The letter *stands* for the sound. The letter does not say anything – except in a metaphorical sense.

One of the snags of ABCs, as has already been mentioned, is that their dependence on pictures makes the use of nouns almost obligatory. Children need to learn other about classes of word, but there are problems in making pictures to accompany words like 'to', 'in', 'at', 'I', 'am', 'my', 'going'. Children have to become acquainted with many such words and the only way this may be done meaningfully is to make sentences in which these words occur. The sentence-making game does just this.

The information about letters and sounds in the picture- and word-matching game must be treated with caution. It is particularly important to recognize that in giving the example 'A for Apple' (where the letter A of Apple corresponds to the short A in the spoken word), this is not the only correspondence between letter A and speech sounds. Letter A also stands for sounds in father, acorn, above, and all; each correspondence for letter A is different in these examples. Because of this, it is as well to give a child the idea of several correspondences rather than one and only one. When a fact is given especially about the vowel letters a, e, i, o, u, it is as well to say something like: 'This is one of the sounds A stands for. It stands for some others too. Today we'll have "A for apple". One day I'll tell you about the others.' With consonants it is easier because there are fewer correspondences to be accounted for; but even here care is needed.

Diane's interest in letters and the sounds they represent was intermittent and her parents neither pressed nor discouraged her pursuit of this kind of information. The letter-shapes game did however stimulate her to ask many questions about letters and another game grew out of this. The idea came from a marriage of two activities. The first happened one day when Diane's mother, in looking for a small screwdriver that had got lost, was clearing out a drawer in the hope of finding it. As all the things were taken out, Diane came to help. She looked with great interest at the variety of objects that came to light: an old fountain pen, some keys, some broken trinkets, a shoe horn, a small bead mat, a set of chop sticks, pieces of sealing wax, a pair of lady's scissors, a small glass shoe, and so on. She gathered together the things that intrigued her most and set them out in front of her. She wanted to know where they came from and what they were for.

DIANE: 'Why does a lady have this kind of scissors?'

MOTHER: 'I think because they're pretty and they're small.'

DIANE: 'They've got little gold bits on them. g.uh* is for gold isn't it?'

MOTHER: 'Yes it is. Like "girl" g.uh.'

DIANE: 'And "sss" is for scissors. What is for shoe?'

MOTHER: 'Sh is for shoe.'

DIANE: 'What is for this?' [*holding up the pen*]

MOTHER: 'p.uh is for pen.'

DIANE: 'p.uh is for pussy as well isn't it? Is "p.uh" for cat as well? No . . . what is for cat?'

MOTHER: 'K.uh is for cat. And for cup.'

DIANE: 'And for saucer . . . Oh no! "sss" is for saucer.'

MOTHER: 'That's right, like scissors.'

DIANE: 'And t.uh is for table.'

MOTHER: 'And d.uh is for Diane.'

DIANE: 'Yes and for daddy. Why isn't "d.uh" for mummy too?'

MOTHER: 'Because "mmm" is for mummy. So let's put all the things back. And I must look for the screwdriver somewhere else.'

This game, a kind of I-spy with objects, became a regular part of her play. She applied the same idea to books like Richard Scarry's *The Best Word Book Ever* and to her own home-made books. The matching of sounds and letters suggested another game which she herself initiated.

One day she said, 'I want to make a "sss" for scissors book.' Her father said, 'That's a good idea. Let's make one. I'll buy you a nice big drawing-book to do it in.' But Diane didn't want a big drawing-book. She showed her father the size she wanted. The next day he brought it home for her and she made the first drawing. It was a pair-of-scissors-like shape, more or less. Her father wrote:

---

*'g.uh'. The sounds associated with letters like g (b, k, d, p, t, in particular) are difficult to make by themselves. Almost inevitably each will be followed by a vowel sound. Thus 'g.uh' if the sound which letter g sometimes stands for followed by the vowel we have written as 'uh'. Notice that the sound associated with letters like s (such as f, m, n, r, l, v) may be pronounced as 's–s–s' or less correctly as 's.uh'. The vowel 'uh' should be avoided where possible.

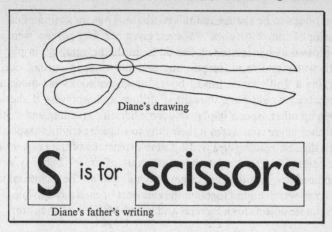

Diane's drawing

S is for **scissors**

Diane's father's writing

Matching cards

He also made a card which Diane could use to match with 'scissors'. On the reverse side of the card he wrote S. He pasted an envelope to the cover of the book for storing the matching cards.

In a few weeks she had made pictures or cut out pictures to illustrate letter-sound relationships. Some of the suggestions for these came from objects and people around her. Some came from her sentence-makings, some from stories. As each picture was finished, the writing was added and a new card was made. The order of items depended entirely on how she selected the items. No one thought of guiding her to use alphabetical order because such an ordering had no useful purpose at this stage.

Diane *played* the matching-game as she played in many other ways during the day. She did what she wanted to do. She was never asked to show her books to visitors, to 'show off' for them. But with sympathetic adults she was likely to ask for a story or for one of her own books to be shared and talked about. Thus no notion of cleverness or of competitiveness was even given her. Her parents were just as pleased at her interest in her dolls, in the new puppy, in playing with water and sand, in painting and drawing, in cutting out, in making a doll's house out of boxes, as in the books she made and read. They would have thought it strange and worrying if she had given up other aspects of play to devote herself to reading and writing and they never considered it their duty to suggest activities associated with this. So reading and writing were extensions of the range of her activities. They took up varying amounts of time – but they never displaced story reading and singing rhymes and all the incidental talk and play which bound together the elements of each day's living.

Suitable objects for a Picture- and Word-Matching Game are:

s	— scissors	x	— box
t	— tree	b and g	— boys and girls
p	— pen	f	— fish-fingers
f	— feather	e	— egg
s	— sausage	h	— hen
m	— mummy	r	— Robert
sh	— shoe	j	— jug
d	— daddy	o and l	— oranges and lemons
ch	— chocolate	z	— zip
m	— mouse	a	— apple
t	— tummy	c and s	— cups and saucers
d, h	— doll's house	th	— thumb
g	— giraffe	th	— thimble
a	— acorn	w	— wolf
p	— penguins	k	— key
e	— envelope	n	— nanny
i	— indians	l	— lady
v	— volcano	y, s	— yellow sun
q	— queen	u	— umbrella

Of course, these are only a few of the possibilities and a more personal home-made version can be made. The cards with the key word on one side and the initial letter on the other, may be made from blank post cards. The handwriting should match that on the pictures as carefully as possible. An envelope stuck to the back of the book, may be used for storing the words.

PICTURES AND WORDS

for the Picture and Word-Matching Game

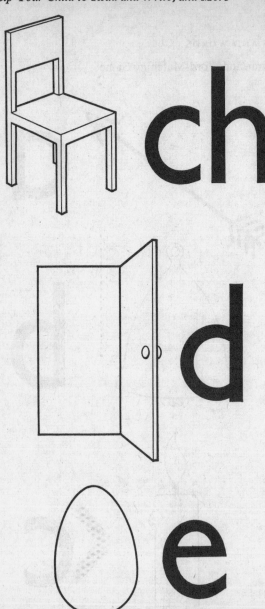

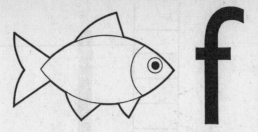

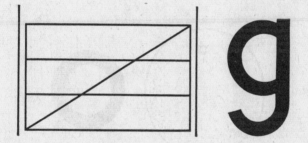

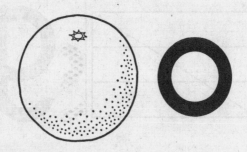

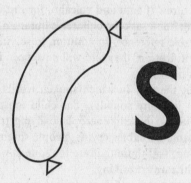

EXAMPLE OF WORD-CARD:

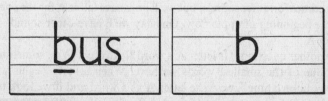

i) face of card   ii) reverse side

How to use the cards:

(1) The pictures and their spoken word labels need to be discussed so that the child knows what each picture represents. Particularly in the case of acorn, cyclist, emu, numbers, ogre, ship, volcano, the items should be talked about so that alternative labels are not confused with those on the card. For instance acorn may be called nut, cyclist – bicycle, emu – bird, numbers – letters or figures, ogre – giant or cave-man, ship – boat, volcano – fire. Answers such as these are sensible and should not be dismissed. Clear explanations of the word which must be associated with each picture should be given after the child has made his suggestions.

(2) Pronounce the word below each picture distinctly and let the child do so as well. Talk about the objects as they are in real life as well as in the pictures. If emu and volcano, for instance, are difficult to find in books at home, ask the children's librarian to help the child to choose a suitable reference. In addition to solving the immediate problems of identification, the child will have been introduced to an important use of books.

(3) Talk about the way in which spoken words are made up of sounds (but not just any sounds). The child must be able to sort sounds into two kinds: those like aeroplanes flying, traffic noises, train whistle, doors banging, babies crying, people singing, dogs barking and radios playing; and those that are the sounds we make with our speech organs while we are talking.

(4) Introduce the letter which represents the speech sound at the beginning of apple. Any questions the child asks should be answered. A difficult one is: 'Why do we have this letter for apple?' The answer might be: 'Well we have to have something to stand for this sound and this shape called letter A is what we use.'

Another question may be: 'What does letter A do?' Answer: 'Well it sometimes stands for the sound at the beginning of apple and sometimes for other sounds, but we'll only have letter A for the sound at the beginning of apple now. One day we'll have other sounds for letter A.'

Another question: 'Is letter A a word?' Answer: 'Yes, sometimes. It's one of the smallest words we have. When a story begins with "once upon *a* time", we write letter A as a word and if we look in a book we'll find quite a lot of them.' Be specially careful when pronouncing the words 'a' to do so naturally, that is, with the sound 'uh' and not 'ay', thus: 'Once upon "uh" time . . .'

(5) To make a set of letter and word cards either draw each letter-word card direct or trace each from pp. 114–16 on to greaseproof paper and then transfer this to pieces of card from household cartons, sweet boxes or shoe boxes – any card with a usable white surface. Alternatively a packet of blank white postcards may be bought. Be careful to see that each letter- or word-card is the size shown on pages 114–16 and that you make all the letter-shapes accurately. There is no need to make all the cards at once. It is a good plan to do this by asking the child which picture he or she would like a matching letter and word-card for. Do this gradually and store the cards as they are made in a used envelope or an empty cigarette packet.

(6) As the cards you have made accumulate, take them out of the envelope in whatever order they come and let the child begin the process of matching. Each match of written word to written word should be accompanied by the pronunciation of the name of each object and then attention should be drawn to the beginning sound and the beginning (underlined) letter of the written word. Thus the letter- and word-card with the word apple on one side and the letter A on the reverse is matched to the picture word page with the same information. The child should finish by thinking about the picture, the spoken word, the written word and its initial letter like this (it will not matter how differently this is expressed so long as the ideas are clear from what the child says):

'This (word) is apple and so is that one.
Apple begins with letter ay.
Letter ay stands for the "a" of apple:
"a" is for apple.'

One possible way of starting is to take the letter with which the child's name begins and compare the item in the picture matching game with his or her name. Other family names may be used in a similar fashion.

As each new card is introduced into the game the child is being offered further examples of information about letters, written words, speech-sounds and spoken words. A proper understanding of what this information consists of may easily escape the child if talk related to the matching process does not take account of the things it is so easy to take for granted. Because the *ideas* the child is learning about are abstract, great care must be taken to make sure that the facts which exemplify these ideas are repeated in new contexts. It may take many separate examples before the child begins to formulate the generalizations which link speech and writing. Each new card is another opportunity for the child to gain further experience of particular instances of the general principles involved.

At first a child may well do no more than repeat information without understanding its significance. Indeed, a true understanding is only possible when many instances have been presented. Gradually over a period of some weeks, the examples will fit together. A child who appears to be making little progress will often suddenly understand as though a missing 'piece' had clicked into place. When this happens he will be ready to use his understanding of the way speech sounds and letters are linked to examples that are not in the game. Just as Diane discovered that Daddy had an initial D (sound and letter) as well as Diane, so children should be encouraged to try making similar discoveries. This may well begin to take place before all the cards, especially the 'alternative value' cards and the two-letter-cards, have been presented. If so, it is a sign that the child has enough information from which to begin to generalize and the rest of the game will be played as fast as he is able to memorize new facts.

(7) The words and pictures are, of course, no more than reminders. They have no special significance and as soon as the child is able to add his own examples to each key word, the place for the game may be taken by the 'I-spy' game. However, notice that whenever this game is played, it uses concrete nouns for its examples. It is as well to make sure the child is able to apply the information he is accumulating to the cards for words like 'the', 'is', 'in', 'at', 'for', 'with', 'my', in the sentence-making game. Because it is, in most cases, impossible to illustrate such words, the child must have reached a clear understanding of how these words are different. The first necessity, then, is to discuss the reason why some words have pictures and some do not have pictures. Second, the non-picture words are not too easy to learn unless they are put into sentences. When they are, the child will often remember them because of the sentences in which they appear.

For example, 'to' and 'for' are clearly related to memorable words in the sentence 'I am going to Butlin's for my holiday.'*

*There is well founded evidence that very young children can learn to recognize words. They have better developed perceptual powers than is popularly believed and in favourable environments, as we have tried to show, thinking and feeling develop at a remarkable pace and as a result children are better adjusted emotionally. Whether very young children *should* learn to recognize words is another matter. G. Doman, an American researcher, thinks they should be given the opportunity to do so and on the basis of his research corroborated by that of other researchers (R. Lynn and H. Diack) he published a kit for this purpose: (in U.K.) *Teach Your Baby to Read*, Jonathan Cape, London, 1965; (in U.S.A.) *How to Teach Your Baby to Read*, Random House, New York, 1964. We believe that at this stage it is *spoken* language which should receive the attention of parents.

13 Children as Writers: Samples of Texts Written by Five- to Seven-Year-Olds

Old-fashioned methods of teaching the piano often meant a long time practising five-finger exercises, scales and arpeggios before ever putting your fingers to a tune, never mind inventing one. Old-fashioned reading and writing were usually taught in a similar way. So much time was spent learning to read lists of words and to write (or transcribe) other people's sentences, that there was none left for using one's own language to put on paper one's own thoughts and feelings. Today, many children learn the art of reading and writing before they are taught much about spelling and handwriting. In doing so they are likely to use texts they have themselves written. They read printed books too but in the early stages they make their own books and share them with other children in the class. They also take them home to read to their parents.

The following texts are all from children in town schools. The first set were taken from early books in which children collected short pieces of writing. During a year these lengthen, increase in number, and gradually fill the page – or several pages. Handwriting improves, spelling matures and sentences flow together with a much better 'fit', as children learn to follow one sentence by others.* Texts vary from child to child, from neighbourhood to neighbourhood. The children in these samples are all making progress in fairly large classes. The writing of children in classes of less than thirty children is indicated. The texts in this chapter are left as they were written. The order in which they appear indicates the age of the child: the youngest come first.

The quality of each text, its subject matter and its use of language

*If a child makes no progress despite the most patient attention, while all the children around him do, he may well need help which the teacher is not trained to give. In such a case, parents should discuss this with the head teacher of the school the child attends.

should be noted. The children's meanings and sentence structures are much more complex than some first reading primers. They are also more able to reflect real life and real people in their writings than the 'professional' reading primers which are often stilted and unreal. (Books with texts which are nearer the qualities of these children's are listed on pages 163–4.)

The Five-Year-Olds

The first set of writings is taken from classes of five years olds over a period of a month. They have just learned how to make written sentences for themselves and are still practising this new skill.

Each sentence is a snippet of experience; many are very ordinary real-life situations: 'I am going to the park with my Nan'. Some are drolleries like 'I am a little hair cut'. Some are make-believe: 'The horse is on the field. We feed it all the time' (this from a child living in a crowded urban area); occasionally one is, on the face of it, disturbing: 'My dad ran away from my mum . . .,' for instance, followed immediately by '. . . and my little brother is going to school'. These young writers are not yet able to express in writing their deeper attitudes and feelings. Indeed many of the children have had little opportunity to discuss their feelings except in the rather public atmosphere of the classroom. This is very different from doing so privately with an adult. Yet with all their limited experience of using written language, these children are creating unselfconscious commentaries on the life around them.

The range of subject matter that interests them is considerable. Under the eye of a sympathetic teacher, talking, spontaneous dramatic play and painting will provide some children with even better ways of coming to terms with experiences than writing can offer them at such a stage in their development.

A great deal has been talked recently about the notion of 'creative writing' and much confusion surrounds this concept. Many people imagine that 'teaching' creative writing means something like the teaching of certain special 'techniques' such as writing 'poetic prose' or using language which is thought to be poetic. Thus children are sometimes encouraged to use many adjectives because it is thought by some teachers that in doing so the children will be writing 'better'.

The use of such 'valuable' words blocks children's creativity as often as it encourages it: their responses are not to their own experience but to how the teacher sees this. In fact creative writing (as opposed to non-creative writing) means leaving each child free to recreate some of his inner world, to formalize his own experience through *his* language. In this sense the following samples of children's writing are a good example of where and how 'creative writing' begins.

SENTENCES COMPOSED BY FIVE-YEAR-OLDS

BILLY:
I can be good for Mrs . . .
my tooth came out yesterday. My little tooth.
my cat is very rough.
my cat catches a mouse.
my baby's name is Paul.
my house is very big.
my tree is very big.
my dog is good.
my new carpet is in my house.
are you a mouse? No.
are you a rabbit? No.
the baby was scratching a match box. My cat is in a very big house.
come here little dog.
the house is burning and the firemen are coming out.
my mum has to tidy the house.

SYLVIA:
I am a big girl.
I am a pretty girl.
I am going to my Nan. I am having a tea party in Nan's house.
my mum is pretty.
I am going to Butlins for my holiday.
I am going to the fun-fair.
I went to my Nan's yesterday.
I played there and I had tea there.
I was sick I stayed in bed.
I am going on a train on Saturday.
I went to the fun-fair yesterday. I saw a fire this morning.
my brother is going to prison.
I was going to school.

I saw the Queen.
I saw the big wheel, and the mousetrap and the big slide.

JACKIE:
it is my birthday on Sunday and I am very lucky.
I am going to Janet's birthday.
soon I am going to Canvey Island and I am going to stay there.
I have got a new dress, and I like it very much.
It was snowing on Sunday and I like the snow.
I have got a new necklace.
I have got a new pretty necklace. I got my new necklace at Tony's.
I am going to Janet's party.
I saw *On the Buses* and the film. I saw *Steptoe* on Monday.
my brother is ill.

TERRY:
once upon a time there lived a witch and she mixed her spells and she fell
    right into the pot and that's the end of her.
I am playing with my toy and I pull it.
go to the fun fair and we have ice cream.
my dog is good and little. My dog is tricky.
we are going on the holiday.
I am going to the park.
I am going to play ball with my friend.
I am a big giant in the world.
I am going in the cage, and I saw the tiger in the cage. I saw the tiger's baby.
we are going in the summer holiday and we went down the road.
this is the fox and he is going in the cottage and he is eating.

JAN (*in a class of less than thirty children*):
I made a book. It is big.
the house and the flower. The rain is making the flower grow.
the children were skiing in school and it was cold.
the farmer works in the fields.

ELIZABETH (*in a class of less than thirty children*):
I like the book. I made this book.
one house is going to fall and one house is strong. (*illustration of two
    houses*)
I am going to the park with my Nan. I am going to my Nan to have a tea
    party. I am going to France.
I saw something about cows on television.

BOB (*in a class of less than thirty children*):
I am a dog.
I am a little chicken.
I am a little hair cut.
look at my little dog's water.
my dad died because he had a heart attack.
my grandmother died because she had a heart attack.
I am a big man come bum. (*sic*)
I am a little clog. (*sic*)
we are going to the chicken bum. (*sic*)
everyday I go to the park.
my mum is going to the house.
I saw the soldier in the castle.

JOHN (*in a class of less than thirty children*):
my favourite book.
my mum has to work all the time.
my mum is getting a new baby for me.
my little brother is coming to school today.
my dad had to work all the time.

SANDY:
my television has conked out.
all the cars are good except Anglias & Escorts.
Queen Elizabeth had passengers in the olden days. It got on fire in Hong
 Kong. Q.E. sank and died. It went under the water.
one day the sun was shining and I said to my mum, go over the park to
 get some fresh air because it was hot.
Mrs . . . is a pretty girl because she has curly hair. I call her blue eyes.

SUE:
I am a girl. I read stories to my mum at home and my dad is silly.
I was asleep last night and my mum came and kissed me, on the lips.
my birthday is on Friday and Karen is not coming but I am going to save
 her some birthday cake.
I went to Simone's christening and I went in a car. I liked the food.
when it is going to be my big brother's birthday he is going to leave me.

HELEN:
my mum is very pretty.
my mum saw a witch up in the sky.
my dad is very strong. My dad and mum lived in the same bed.

my friend is driving a car.
my mum likes cats.
my mum don't like dogs.
my dad is very lazy and my mum used to get up very early.
my dad likes a cup of tea.

JUNE:
my mum is very nice.
jump up.
the home is very big.
come in little kitten.
my mum comes in and jumps.
my mum did my hair.
a sweet shop I wanted.
I like my baby.
I went to the sweet shop.
my mum is working very hard.
my dad stole jewels.
Lee is kissing.

BARRY:
my mum is very big.
my mum is getting a new baby.
my dad has to work all the time.
my dad has to take my mum to work in the car.
we had to go in the sweet shop.
my mum has to stay at home all the time. My mum bought some sweets.
I like my little dog and his name is Sheba. I like it all the time.
the horse is on the field. We feed it all the time and my horse likes it on the field.
the workmen are in the home, and they are painting the house.
we went to the airport and we saw a jumbo jet and we saw Paul's aeroplane and it was very good.
the workmen are finished and they are doing the kitchen and they are painting.
I have a magic box and it is magic. It is very magic and it is very big.

JOYCE:
on Saturday I am going to get my new shoes.
I am a pattern.
why do robbers rob a bank? Because they want money.
my grandad died because he had a heart attack.

my brother has got a James Bond Beach Buggy.
my grandmother died because she had a heart attack.
I have got my new shoes and my brother went mad.
my brother was greedy.
one day a boy jumped so high that he fell flat in the duck pond.
I am going to a farm and I saw some cows.

STEVE:
my pretty house.
the mice are crawling in the kitchen.
I like Lee.
I go jumping and the big shop.
I like my dad.
my dad is strong.
my dad has a car in a garage.
my cat catches a mouse.
my sister is on the couch.
I like my dad's car.
my dog catches mice and eats them all up.

ALLAN:
my mum and dad. (*picture of a big car under the sun*).
my mum and dad go to work on time.
my dad and mum lived in an old house.
my dad ran away from my mum and my little brother is going to school.
my dad ran to a robber's camp. He got shot by the robbers.
I am going to see my new house on Sunday.
my mum likes a job and she likes it very much.

Of 142 sentences written by these children, 114 have as subject 'I' or 'my . . .' (and another 5 deal with 'we'). Thus more than 80 per cent of the sentences have subject-matter directly concerning the child himself ('I am . . .') or someone or something closely related to him ('My dad, cat, sister . . .'). In fact, because sentences which are very similar are not included here, the percentage of 'I' and 'My' sentences is actually more than 90 per cent. Sentences like 'One day a boy jumped so high that he fell flat in the duck pond' which move away from a completely egocentric view of the world towards an involvement in objective reality, are, at this stage, written by few children.

The Six-Year-Olds

The following pieces by six-year-olds show these children acquiring literary voices true to themselves. They are also experimenting with how they may use their writing skills.

SENTENCES COMPOSED BY SIX-YEAR-OLDS

JANICE:
I like my orange dress.
my black and red kilt I like it.
I like my red dress.
I have got my bell bottoms on.
I like my orange jumper.

DONELLY:
When we have holidays I play out on Sunday.
I play with my toys.
I like my holidays.
We went to the sea side.
When I got there the sea came to me.
It went back again. I chased it.
When the water went back in its place it came again.

MARY:
Mrs H . . . is in hospital because she likes to give her blood away.
Mrs H . . . is putting her blood in the bottle.
The Dr went to his room to give the bottles to the sick people.
The nurse brought Mrs H . . . a cup of tea and a biscuit.
Mrs H . . . came home. She had a bandage on her arm.
Mrs H . . . told her children that she went to hospital to give her blood away.

EDWARD:
Once upon a time there lived a fly he was daddy fly in a family. There was one girl and no boys.
The daddy went to get some food for the girl and the mammy. The fly went to a ladies house.
She got some special stuff to kill it but the daddy fly got away and had some food.

LOU:

Once upon a time there lived a prince and a princess.

And they got lost but the prince knew the way back and how they lived happily ever after.

Once upon a time there lived a dragon and a brave knights.

The dragon puffed out some smoke luckily it missed them and now they lived happily ever after.

ROGER:

Once upon a time there lived a dragon and he was very harmless, and he was burning houses and one day a knight came to fight the dragon and the dragon fired smoke but it missed and the knight killed the dragon and they lived happily ever after

A NOTE ON 'BREAKTHROUGH TO LITERACY'

These sentences composed by five- and six-year-olds were selected from the work of children who are using *Breakthrough to Literacy* materials.

Breakthrough Reading Books are now published in Puffin Books but these form only part of the materials. From the point of view of the learner the keys to *Breakthrough* are the Sentence Maker and the Word Maker by means of which children are able to compose written sentences and to study the way written words are made. Reference to *Breakthrough to Literacy* is made in *The Language of Primary School Children* by Connie and Harold Rosen,* Chapter 4, pp. 157 ff. A more extensive description of *Breakthrough to Literacy*, including comments on the Programme and its theoretical basis will be found in Pat D'Arcy's *Reading for Meaning, Volume 1, Learning to Read,*† chapter VI, pp. 118 ff.

The following excerpts taken from the introduction to the teacher's manual‡ will give, we hope, a clear idea of what *Breakthrough to Literacy* is and how it works:

*Published by Penguin Education for the Schools Council, Harmondsworth, 1973.

†Published by Hutchinson Educational for the Schools Council, London, 1973.

‡*Breakthrough to Literacy Teacher's Manual*, Longman, London, 1970 (new edition 1975).

The crux of Breakthrough to Literacy is the Sentence Maker. This is a three-page folder in which there is room to store about 200 words. On two of the pages 130 of the words most commonly used by children have been printed. These are also printed on white cards which the teacher stores centrally in the classroom. Each word on white card fits into a pocket and covers the same word printed on the Sentence Maker itself. The third page also has pockets for words but it is unprinted. This is so that each child may ask for words that do not appear on the printed pages. The teacher is provided with strips of ruled white card on which to write such words.

Each printed word has to be carefully matched into its place after use. By doing this each child practises word recognition (with high frequency for certain words) and learns to become more and more discriminating in how he sees printed words. This is an important but incidental feature of the Sentence Maker in use. Each child will begin to use his individual Sentence Maker after a period of careful training on the large Teacher's Sentence Maker. At the beginning, his own Sentence Maker will have about twelve to fifteen printed word cards and one hand-written word card with his name. These he has learned to use with the teacher. He must now learn to use them on his own. He will add new words gradually but always in consultation with the teacher.

To make sentences, he selects words from the Sentence Maker and slots them into a small plastic stand. In this way he sets out to match a sentence he has structured 'in his head' with a printed version in his stand.

Having made his sentence, the child is then invited to read it aloud and when the teacher and the child are both satisfied, the teacher writes it into the child's Sentence Book. In this way there is a permanent record of the child's work. He is, in fact, writing his own book. He will illustrate this afterwards if he chooses.

Take for example, some sentences produced after a few weeks' use of Breakthrough to Literacy:

I am a pretty girl
I went to Nan's yesterday
I played there and I had tea there
I was sick I stayed in bed.

The quality that shows through these sentences is very like that of children's spoken language and only a little more formal, a little more self-conscious ... The short sentences which children start to compose will gradually grow in length and complexity.

Handwriting is not overlooked. The teacher is encouraged to help children to gain fluent, legible handwriting without this interfering with their sentence making. Handwriting is seen as a skill which serves to enable the child to do more of the business of composing sentences for himself.

As both a reader and a writer the child needs to have a knowledge of spelling. To help him with this we have produced the Word Maker, a two-page folder with pockets like the Sentence Maker. Consonant symbols are printed on one page (e.g.: b, c, d, f, etc. but also ch, sh, th, etc.) and simple vowel symbols on the other (e.g.: a, e, i, o, u, y). White printed cards are inserted into the appropriate pockets and these are selected by the child to make written words. The Word Maker is used to discover how words are constructed from written symbols.

Other components of *Breakthrough to Literacy* are:

(1) Sally go round the sun: a set of 46 nursery rhymes on cards and an L.P. record on which each nursery rhyme is spoken and sung (where there is a traditional tune available).

(2) The Magnet Board and figurines are designed to help children who have not had enough experience of expressing in language the relationships that exists between people, places and objects.

(3) (a) Breakthrough Books are intended to be read to children and discussed with them before they are read by children themselves.

    (b) Big Breakthrough Books: About the House and an ABC for hungry girls and boys.

    (c) Breakthrough Lollipops are collections of poetry and rhymes in four books dealing with people, birds, animals and weather.

The Seven-Year-Olds

Next, some longer pieces by seven-year-olds. These are the children who have 'taken off'. Their literacy is developing rapidly. They read well and enjoy the books in school and from their local children's library. The confidence with which these children write about themselves is one major change for which educational practice is entirely responsible. This is not something that happens by accident – under the experienced guidance of teachers, children learn how to 'wrestle with words', how to master their abilities to record their thoughts and feelings. In so doing they are given opportunities for coming to terms with experience and increasing the skill with which they use their mother tongue.

The transcriptions which follow reproduce the spellings of the originals.

STORIES COMPOSED BY SEVEN-YEAR-OLDS

MARTIN:

Once upon a time there lived an old man, he had no little boys and girls or a wife, he lived in a little cottage he had only one dog and nothing else and he cooked his sausage in a pot because he was so poor and he had to eat grass for his tea and he had to drink adams ayl [ale] he had to sleep on a dirty rubber rug because he didn't have a bed. He had no chair or tables, one day he was 80.

My Wedding by ANDREA:

Last week we had a wedding in our classroom I got married to Tariq.

I wore a long white dress and I wore a lacy veil and I made some flowers out of tissue paper.

Tariq wore a tall hat made out of blue paper.

Mrs . . . gave him a flower to put in his buttonhole.

He looked very nice and I looked very nice too.

I had three bridesmaids. They were Sanorina and Tracey and Alison. Robert was the best man, Mark was the vicar. After the wedding Tariq kissed me.

JOE:

Once upon a time there lived a king called King Arthur, he lived in Camelot. His knights did good deeds for their country.

Their enemies were black knights. King Arthur had a beautiful sword and a beautiful crown too. He was a good king.

When King Arthur was old remember the lady in the pond said when you die you must give back your sword.

He was very brave. It is very tricky because there can be people on the trees and they shoot at you.

The ships were funny. Some of the knights are called Real force men [reinforcement].

If some one wants to Eskat [escape] they kill a man put his clothes and and go away.

They no how was on there sade bekos they had a picer on there sheel [they know who was on their side because they had a picture on their shield].

They had armour. There were princess and princes, that had there heads chop of.

BRENDA:

Once upon a time there lived a King and a Queen and they lived in a very old castle.

The Queen's name was Queen Victoria and the King's name was King Charles.

King Charles kept on having fights and many men was killed. Soon King Charles was Over taken and all off King Charles men were in prison.

Then one day Queen Victoria laid a baby and all the other Kings men wanted to kill the baby but Queen Victoria did not want her baby to be killed. So she hided the baby

under her skirt. The baby would not stop tickling her legs and Queen Victoria could not stop laughing and the guards said why are you laughing. I think your nose is like a sausage said Queen Victoria.

all the People laughed at the guards and they all for got to look for the baby and they went some were else and King Charles hit the gards head and got the keys.

My Baby Sister by LOUIS:

One day Mum went into hospital, to have a baby.

We had been waiting for her for a very long time.

Months and months.

Dad and I went to hospital to fetch them home.

The baby was ever so small smaller than Peter Brown's puppy.

About like our guinea pigs.

When we got home, Mum put her in the Carry cot.

Then she gave her a bottle of milk.

I held the bottle with Mum.

When we took the bottle away she yelled ever so loud.

I put my hands over my ears.

Mum picked her up and patted her back.

That did the trick – she dropped off to sleep with her fingers in her mouth.

Mum said I used to do that,

but I don't believe her.

When it is sunny, Mum puts her in the pram in the front garden.

'You boys keep quiet now. Ann's asleep'.

It makes you fed up sometimes.

Some days Mum takes her to the clinic.
That's a laugh.
All these babies in their rests kicking and screaming.
Poked about by the nurse.
On the scales – just like we weigh our guinea pigs.

MARY:
I saw lots of gold and silver
   And gold is the colour of the sun
   And silver is the colour of the rain
   And I saw rubies
   And diamonds
   And a ruby is the colour of a rose.
   And a diamond is the one with all the colours.

14 Reading: Spelling It Out, or Looking and Saying?

Not so long ago it would have been general to find young children taught the alphabet as a starting point for learning to read. From this they would have learned to spell two- and three-letter words and finally they would read these in specially prepared reading primers.

The methods evolved from this approach to reading still linger on – especially where chi¹dren are taught at home. There are, however, other approaches but controversy about reading centres mainly on two of these. The first puts forward claims for teaching letters and their associated sounds (phonics). The weakness in building a total approach to reading in this way is well illustrated by typical 'primer' sentences like these:

Dan can fan Nan
The man is on the log
The pig is in the pen
The hen is on the box
The ox is in the bog

The second argument makes different claims. In reacting strongly against the alphabetic and the spelling method, the supporters of the sound and sight method (the 'look-say' method) claimed that children could be taught to recognize words after these had been shown and pronounced many times. But the need for repetition in the writing of texts for use with this method produced its own kind of abnormal sentences:

Look, Look. See the kitty
See the Kitty Tom.
See the Kitty.
Oh! Look! Kitty has the ball –
Look, Tom, look.
Look at the Kitty.

For a time teachers who used this method believed that they had found an escape from the strange language associated with spelling methods and that they had found a new way to involve children in what they learned to read. That this was not so is illustrated by the following story.

One day a six-year-old boy paid his first visit to the zoo. The next day he described some of the animals that had impressed him. He became very excited about the lion he had seen. 'I saw this great big lion and when the man came to feed him, he opened his mouth and boy, did he roar . . . !' The teacher was very pleased with his 'story' and said she would write it down for him. Following the 'look and say' approach, she wrote: 'See the lion, Oh! Oh! Oh!'

A little bit of experience recollected in normal, expressive language, was reduced to well-meant nonsense.

Many teachers try to use three-letter words to show how three separate letters can represent three speech-sounds fused together. The separate letters of which written words are made do not of course represent separate sounds since the sounds which make up spoken words flow together into each other, so that it is difficult to say where any except the first sound begins or where any except the last ends. (Few words are made up of single sounds: 'I', 'a', 'oh', 'ah' are rare examples.) In written words the letters never *fuse* in this way. This is an important point for children to grasp. However, it is hardly necessary to limit children to words of three, two and one letters to make the point clear. There has been much controversy about this in the teaching of reading. The weakness in the argument for using short words is easily illustrated by looking at sentences constructed of 'little words'. Take for example the following 'primer' sentences:

The man in on the log.
The pig is in the pen.
The hen is on the box.
The ox is in the bog.

Such language is far from the experience of any speaker of English. Sentences such as these never occur outside the artificial boring world of many reading primers. It has no connection with children's experience of language or of life, its meaning is difficult to reach even at second hand, while all the richness of first-hand experience is set aside. It is indeed not for its *meaning* that such language is used, but because it affords children practice in reading words with spelling patterns that they are expected to master or in recognizing words after they have been seen many times. This confusion between *spelling practice* and *reading practice* is the major weakness of such teaching materials, though some writers do have a great flair for involving the reader in the meaning of a story concocted out of such limited means, as the following excerpt demonstrates:

A PET DOG
A bad boy had a dog. The dog was not a bad dog, but the boy was a bad boy, for he was bad to his dog.

If I see a boy do ill to any one who is not as big as he is, or to a dog, or cat, or ass, or cow, and say it is 'for fun' I say it is 'bad fun', and in the end the bad boy may see it was bad fun, yes, and sad fun for him too. So now, as I did say to you the bad boy was bad to his dog; for oft he hit his dog, and his dog had not a bed to lie on, and oft he had not a bit to eat.

I saw the bad boy one day hit his dog and say 'Ha, ha, ha! you bad dog; ha, ha, Sir! get out of my way, I say. I hit you, yes, and I can hit you, for you are my own dog, and no one can say me nay.'

And so he hit his dog, – and all 'for fun' as he did say. He hit him so oft, the dog did cry, and cry, and in the end the dog did fly at the bad boy and bit him in the leg. And now it was for the bad boy to cry; yes, to cry out and say, 'Oh! my leg, my leg, Oh! the bad, bad dog, Oh! oh! oh!'

And no one was sad for the bad boy; but all did say, 'Fie! fie! Why did you hit the dog? It was not the dog who was bad, but you!'

Oh! how the bad boy did vex me!

This is surely a brilliant performance – in some ways akin to constructing a musical form out of three notes. But for all his sheer cleverness the author cannot disguise the abnormality of his language.

Compare this with the work of a six-year-old boy writing in 1972:

OUR BLACK KITTEN
my friend Martin has a big black cat called Apple
one day she had 5 Kittens.
Martin let me look at them,
all curled up in a box,
soft and black,
eyes shut.
"can I have one?".
run home fast, and ask mum.

"yes, if you keep it downstairs.
I'll have no cats upstairs
in my house".
one day Martin came to our house
with a box.
"look inside, Dave"
yes, a soft black thing,
a moving black thing.
a soft black kitten for me.
find a box.
make him cosy with an old coat.
"come here, Blackie.
come to your new bed,
your soft warm bed".
"give him some milk"
said mum.
"here's your milk, Blackie.
drink it up".

In this writing there is no restriction placed on the child from the teacher or the text-book writer. The child is using all the words he needs and his sentences show his response to the way he and those around him use language. This does not mean that his teacher is not offering him the opportunity to learn about spelling in an orderly fashion. It *does* mean that spelling is not all he is learning. He is also learning about how to make a coherent text in natural English, which is something *he cannot learn from practising spelling*.

Letters and the sounds they represent may be practised without putting anyone's 'ox in the bog' and word recognition is not mastered simply by repeating a word frequently. Children must be motivated to learn to read by the interest the text creates for them: reading methods which only permit them to have a limited view of the act of reading are both dangerous and discouraging because they leave the child so much to learn on his own.

A growing number of schools have in recent years helped children to begin reading and writing by making books like Diane – using their own experiences as a starting point. Children have also had many stories told to them and read to them so that they know the language of story-telling. In this way their learning is supported by their own language, experiences and interests.

15   First Books for Children to Read for Themselves

Not all the books in this chapter can be found in book-shops because some are only sold direct to schools. If the details are given to a book-shop, they can usually order them. Local playgroups can often help parents who have difficulty in obtaining books and play materials.

Long before they are ready for 'reading books' children may have begun to recognize words from a variety of sources including lines from nursery rhymes, the labels in books like Richard Scarry's, some headings in a book on trains, the ingredients in a children's cook-book, animal picture books, ABCs. But when they begin to read sentences as opposed to words the books they are given should use language which is relevant to them and which is like their own language. Most people would think mother crazy if she set out to help her baby's incipient language to develop by speaking sentences like: 'Look at the cat. Oh! Oh! Oh!' or 'Nan's pan is gone. Is Nan's fan in the pan? No the man has Nan's fan'. Yet surprisingly enough, many people react very differently when their children are given such nonsensical stuff in reading primers, and do not realize that to offer children boring, meaningless language may well create a strong aversion to reading altogether.

Parents should choose early reading books in the same way as they choose picture story books. The pictures, the text and the ideas which any book contains should be judged by the highest standards.

Until children are beginning to feel confident about reading, the books they are given from this list should be read to them, not just once.

Most of the following books are no more than sixteen pages long. The illustrations support the text and the young reader has the satisfaction of being able to read a whole book in a relatively short time. The renewal of interest which each new book brings will be encouraged by the pictures each different artist provides and by the different subject matter the authors write about.

First Reading Books

LEILA BERG (editor), *Little Nippers*, Macmillan, London.

When *Little Nippers* first appeared they created a considerable stir in educational circles because they dared to consider the quality of urban life and to depart from the cardboard figure of 'school readers' with their stereotyped pictures of families and of childhood. They are not all equally good, but they are all worth considering. The subject matter is varied and often humorous and the writing lively and authentic, while the illustrations at their best are as good as those in the best picture story books.

DICK BRUNA, *I Can Read*, Methuen, London, 1969.

A very simple text illustrated in the very personal 'chunky' style of this author-artist.

VARIOUS AUTHORS, *Early I Can Read Books*, *I Can Read Books*, World's Work, London.

A very imaginatively written and boldly illustrated set of books. Children will soon establish their favourites among the titles now available. A children's librarian will help in choosing the best stories.

VARIOUS AUTHORS and ILLUSTRATORS, *Breakthrough Reading Books*, Puffin, Harmondsworth; Bowmar Publishing, Glendale.

The books are varied in subject matter and illustrations. Many of them are based on stories told by children to the authors or are modelled on sentences made by children. The yellow series of *Breakthrough Reading Books* contain sentences very like those children will make for themselves.

JUNE MELSER, *Read It Yourself Books*, Methuen Educational, London, 1972.

These little books have simple repetitive texts which fulfil the expectations raised by the general series title.

BEVERLEY RANDELL (photographed by Penn Mckay), *Methuen Instant Readers*, Methuen Educational, London; Bowmar Publishing, Glendale.

BEVERLEY RANDELL and CONRAD FRIEBOE, *Methuen Caption Books*, Methuen, London.

More little books with well devised repetitive texts, some with questions and answers. Further additions to this series have been published recently with illustrations by Jill McDonald. Methuen *Number-Story Caption Books* are very simply and effectively illustrated and present ideas about size, shape and counting very clearly.

JENNY TAYLOR and TERRY INGLEBY, *This Is the Way I Go*, Longman, 1965.

Colourful illustrations accompany simple texts which describe how certain creatures run, fly, jump, crawl, climb and swim.

16 Handwriting

What It's About

There are many different ways in which letters may be written and printed. Children need limits placed on the variations in letter-shapes they are introduced to. Publishers of recent books for children to read for themselves usually take great care to see that the texts they publish have letter-shapes which are very close to the script most commonly used by teachers in infant schools.

This chapter is intended as a summary of what a child needs to know in order to produce a fluent script. It sets up a model for use at home and from which help may be given to a child at the appropriate time. We show how, in the pre-writing stage, children begin to work with patterns which prepare them for writing letter-shapes. When children are ready for writing proper – the two stages may well overlap – they need guidance in how best to write letter-shapes. This is provided in the series of diagrams which show the direction of the strokes which make up each letter.

A careful look at Patrick's handwriting version of *Roy the Boy* (see pp. 218–24) will show that he has a very unorthodox handwriting style. He uses combinations of upper- and lower-case letter-shapes as the fancy takes him. Yet this in no way lessens the impact of his story. He had worked out for himself a way of writing fast. Not many children achieve the speed with which Patrick was able to write over lengthy stretches of text untroubled about the spelling of words. Most of the time both his handwriting and his spelling are easily understood.

It would have been wrong to interfere with him on either score. A few months later, however, he took up his story again to read to some family friends, his ideas had changed and he considered many of his spellings 'funny'. His handwriting too had become more conventional. At the same time he had also begun to conform to the expectations of his teacher in the amount he wrote: he now produced no more than a page or two at most.

. It is a matter of some delicacy to decide how best to help a child; help given in one area may become a hindrance in another. There is not much value in arriving at perfect spelling and handwriting if there is nothing worth while to do with them. Provided the child is moving consistently towards a mature model of the *conventions* of written language and is at the time producing written texts which are filled with his awareness of himself and life around him, we can be sure that he is somehow receiving all the help in the skills that he needs.

Patrick had incidental help whenever he asked for it – sometimes from his parents and sometimes from his elder brother. He knew what to do when he needed to know something. He had learned how to formulate a problem and then to get help in solving it from any-one who had time to spare him. Knowing what to do when faced with a problem is an important part of knowing what it is to be a learner – *of knowing how to learn.*

Young children can be as creative in working out a system of handwriting as in anything else which challenges them. One five-year-old worked patiently at handwriting movements in which he moved the paper while his pencil made sharp movements to and fro: ingenious, but slow and cumbersome. Yet he continued to write like this for some days despite the fact that other children around him were writing in a more conventional manner. His teacher wisely showed him an easier method of making letter-shapes. Diane's mother did much the same. In effect she said: 'This is how I do it. Now you have a go. You try.' Until the child experiences the nature of the activity in a practical and experimental manner he has no way of knowing *in himself* what the activity is nor of knowing whether he can do it himself. The earliest attempts may be only an approxi-mation to the example that has been offered, yet these can be very satisfying because involvement in a mysterious act begins to remove the mystery and to make us its master. From the first successful attempts, writing is never again a mystery.

But (like everything else about written language) there is much to learn about the way letters are formed by means of delicate wrist and finger movements. A child who is able to control a pencil only with arm movements is not ready to learn much about handwriting. But like Diane, he may begin by painting large letter-shapes. This will be enough to establish a rudimentary notion of what it feels like to write. But there is much more to handwriting than just making letter-shapes.

When children are introduced to handwriting, they are, very properly, left free to make letter-shapes as large as they wish. They are not at this stage restricted in any way and while they experiment with hand and arm movements it is inevitable that they will need to pass from large rather gross movements to smaller refined movements. The necessary muscular control will not come only from painting, drawing and writing. All manipulative activities – such as building with bricks, catching a ball, playing with toy trains, cutting out pictures to stick in a home-made book – contribute to the child's general ability to control all the muscles of his arms, especially those he eventually learns to use in handwriting.

The Writing Line

Although most printed texts are set down on unlined paper, the horizontals formed by the printed words conform to an invisible division of the letter space. The same is true of handwriting on blank paper. Printer's type and handwritten letter-shapes are designed to fit the writing line in a certain prescribed manner so that the eye may receive visual information in the most economic manner. To achieve this, the greater part of the information supplied by each letter-shape is carried in the centre of the writing line (A) in the diagram. Above this there is space for the ascending strokes (B) on certain letters; below there is space for the descending strokes (C).

The writing line is divided into three portions:

space for ascenders

space for body of letters

space for descenders

In practice the three spaces are used like this:

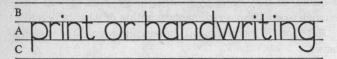

Old-fashioned copy books (in which much unnecessary hand-writing practice used to take place) were generally ruled up in this way. Because of their misuse in schools they were rejected as a class-room aid and with them, the visual presentation of the way the writing line is divided up, which can be very helpful to children. Children do of course discover it for themselves in time (and even if they knew about it from the beginning they would not be able to use the information until they had considerable experience of writing out their own sentences). But it is not wise to assume that they will know about this when they need to and it certainly wastes time discovering it by trial and error. A convention such as this is easily demonstrated and made available to the child, when he is ready to make use of such information.

SPACES BETWEEN WRITING LINES

Each writing line must have space above it and below it to ensure that printed or handwritten words will be surrounded on all sides by enough space to keep them from touching, thus:

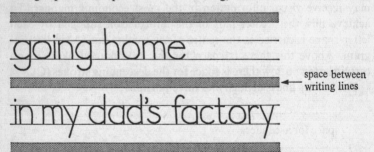

space between writing lines

PAGE MARGINS

The distribution of writing lines on a printed page is controlled by margin space. Pictures are allowed to go into the margins and across two pages. This does not usually happen with the text which is set within margins which will be standard for each page:

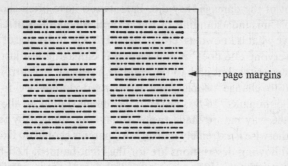

page margins

The various uses of spacing are important in written texts. Controlling all of them is a difficult task for the young child. He has to ensure that:

(1) his page has appropriate margins within which he will set down his text.
(2) his writing lines are horizontal within these margins.
(3) his letters have letter spaces between them.
(4) his words have consistent word spaces between them.
(5) his sentences have consistent sentence spaces between them.
(6) the writing lines have consistent line spaces between them.

Children do not easily manage to control all these until they have had considerable practice in writing their own texts. They will take longer to do so if left to find them out for themselves. Discussion of the physical aspects of a book, including the lay-out of the pages, will help them to understand what they themselves must do as writers. In making writing clear and pleasing to look at it is the reader who is being considered. If no one takes much interest in the child's efforts writing will soon not matter much to him. Having sympathetic and involved readers is something all writers need.

Making Letter-Shapes

The direction of writing from left to right suits the right-handed more comfortably than the left-handed. It used to be thought necessary to force the latter to conform to the practice of the majority 'for their own good'. Many unfortunate people were punished by sarcasm, intolerance and many a smack by teachers who were ignorant of the damage they did. Parents too have often shown remarkable misunderstanding of the natural functioning of children who have what is known as 'cross-laterality'. The insistence of 'doing what everyone else does' in this respect is damaging not just to the child as a writer, but also to the child as a person. It is arrogant to attempt to change people from left-handed dominance to right-handed dominance. In this respect all children should be allowed to follow the way nature made them. Today any attempt by teachers to do otherwise is extremely unlikely. All parents should do likewise.

The following descriptions are for the right-handed. Left-handed children must be taught to make letter-shapes in the most comfortable and economic way. There are more ways than one of holding a pen or pencil and of constructing handwritten letters. If a method proves cumbersome and hence slow and tiring, then experiments with other methods should be tried until one that suits the individual is found. An older left-handed writer from a local primary school might be invited to demonstrate handwriting for the parents and the young learner to see how the writing position and method of holding pen or pencil need to change to suit the left-handed.

WRITING POSITION

The young child is happy to write anywhere, with paper or blackboard in any position – on his knees, on the floor, on a table. He may also position himself awkwardly in relation to the writing surface and develop awkward letter shapes on this account alone. Although one does not wish to curb the enthusiasm which causes a child to seize a pencil and begin to write, there is no great gain in being impromptu if one is also uncomfortable.

The child should therefore be able to sit so that his forearms can rest on the table horizontally. The position of the paper should not cause him to have to bend forward. Nor should it cause him to twist his writing arm out of alignment. The forearm should be able to move across the paper easily without the rest of the body having to move. As the lines of writing descend on the page, the non-writing hand may be used to hold the paper in position and to move it further back on the table so that the writing arm does not need to be moved back too far. As the writing nears the bottom of the page, the paper should be moved up so that the side of the hand rests on the table. None of this is obvious: some children will move themselves rather than the paper. They sometimes also begin to write on a cluttered surface without bothering to clear enough space for their paper. Try to train children to clear a space for themselves and, if the surface of a table is not smooth, to write on a newspaper spread under the writing paper.

Writing may also be done on a sloping surface but again the position of the writer's arm and hand should give him maximum freedom and comfort.

POSITION AND SIZE OF LETTERS ON THE WRITING LINE

Early writing by children often ignores the way in which letter size should remain roughly constant throughout a handwritten text. The examples on pages 189–94 show this. Children also find it difficult to keep the writing line horizontal and hence to position each letter on the appropriate part of the writing line. It is to help with such problems that ruled exercise books are *sometimes* used. However, this is by no means the solution to the problem. The ruled line is a suggestion (or an invitation) the young child may easily ignore because he does not understand its significance; or he may simply have too little manual control to be able to – even if he wants to. The provision of ruled lines is therefore not necessarily of any help at all – the more so if the child has had very little opportunity to start with large, free brush letters and gradually reduce letter size as his control increases. Allow him to *choose* whether he uses ruled or blank paper and encourage him to experiment with both. But first he should know what he is supposed to do and for this he needs to hear about it, to ask questions about it and to watch demonstrations of what he is eventually required to do himself.

HOLDING THE PENCIL

The use of thumb, first and second fingers to hold the pencil in position will have been mastered by a child who has abandoned other less satisfactory methods of holding brushes, crayons and felt pens. By the time he needs to write, he will probably know the best way to hold a writing tool. A child who has never been allowed to scribble or paint, however, will not know this and will need plenty of experience with these before he is ready for the business of making letter-shapes.

Sometimes a child will hold a pencil with a very tight grip, as though it would otherwise escape from him. This is frequently accompanied by too much pressure on the paper. The resulting writing cuts into the surface of the paper and may even tear it. Whatever the cause of such tension, it is obviously a strain on the muscles used to move the pencil and the child should be shown how to apply light pressure with an equally lightly held pencil so that he can make flowing shapes. A good-quality pencil should be used with a thick soft black grade of lead. This allows written marks to be made with very gentle pressure.

THE MOVEMENTS THAT MAKE LETTER SHAPES

Much of the description of letter shapes in chapter 9 applies also to the handwritten forms of letters. There may be divided into three main groups:

(1) those made entirely of straight lines and slants.
(2) those which incorporate an anti-clockwise circular movement.
(3) those which incorporate a clockwise circular movement.

The making of circular shapes is something the children will have used in many different contexts – a circle as a sun, a ball, the human head, the centre of a flower shape and so on. In none of these is it of importance whether the circle is made clockwise or anti-clockwise. In making letter-shapes like b and d this is no longer the case:

Letters made with anti-clockwise movement	Letters made with clockwise movement
c, a, d, g, q, e, o, (s), u.	b, p, n, m, h, r, (s).

Pre-writing Patterns

In painting and drawing, children find ways of making patterns which are based on similar movements to those which make up letter-

rain:

smoke:

dots:

spirals on a snail:

umbrellas open-closed:

pin men:

curves:

long lines:

short lines:

lines and dots:

sun:

(small)   (large)

circle (ball)
and short lines:

circle (ball)
and long lines:

curves (moon):

lines and curves (bridges):

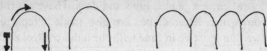

upside down (waves):

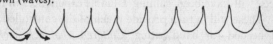

snakes:

umbrella tops:

zig zag:

kisses:

another zig zag:

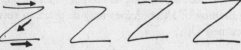

circles and tails:

shapes, loops, curves, jagged lines and dots. These are the basic elements from which letter-shapes are also made. Preparing children for handwriting must be in tune with the hand control each child has mastered. Children who have had the opportunity to cut and paste, to construct collages, to make models from waste materials, to work with scraps of wood, to weigh and measure, to sort and arrange small objects, will have been gaining valuable experiences in manipulative skills. These will in turn provide much of the controlled hand movement needed for handwriting. *Children who lack such experience should not be presented with handwriting exercises of any kind before this serious omission has been made good.*

Pre-writing patterns may be linked to what children already know concerning natural shapes.

Handwriting diagrams

Handwriting should, in the early stages, be concerned with two things: firstly, the shape of each letter, and secondly, the direction of movements of pencil or crayon in making each letter. Letter-shapes at this stage should be made as large as possible. They may be traced in a sand tray before permanent writing takes place. A flat baking tray filled with fine, dry, clean sand is an excellent medium in which finger tracing and later, tracing with a stick may be practised.

Each letter-shape in the sets of drawings which follow is set out to show its position on the writing line, as well as the directions of each of the movements that complete its shape. Position will be mastered at a later stage and to begin with children will make letters which vary in size and in position on the writing line. *Until they have a good deal of experience in writing words and sentences for themselves no lines should be used to guide them.* (See the examples of handwriting on pages 188–94. See also *Talking about letter-shapes*, pages 118–19.)

Thus the making of letter-shapes may be seem to result from decisions concerned with:

(1) ideas about the shape of the letter to be made,
(2) information about where to begin making each letter shape,
(3) information about the kinds of lines which make up the letter,
(4) information about when to change the direction in which a line must go.

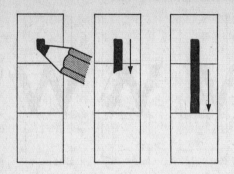

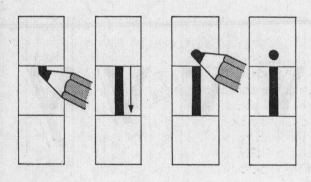

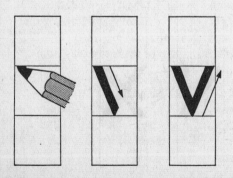

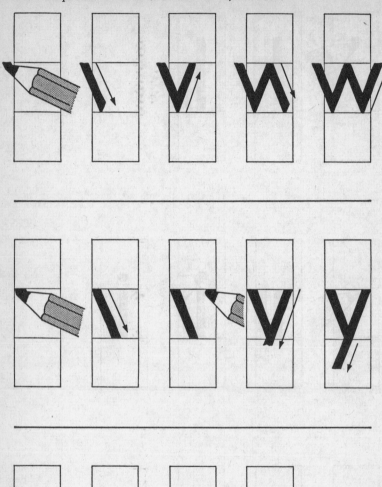

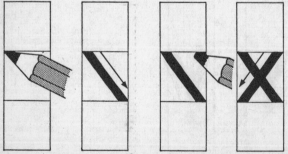

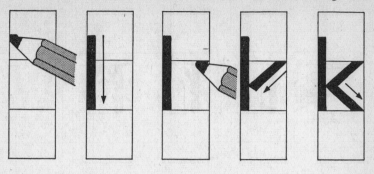

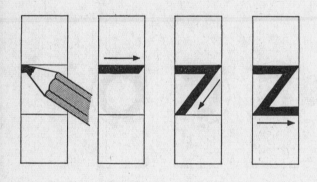

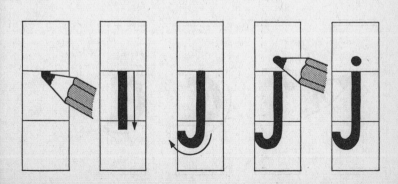

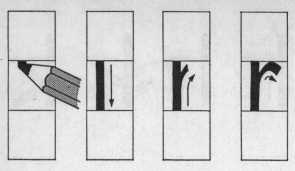

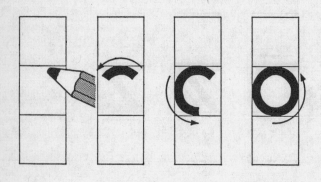

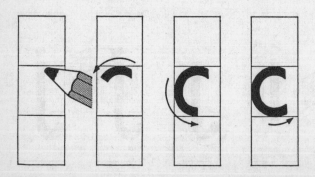

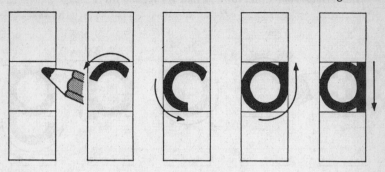

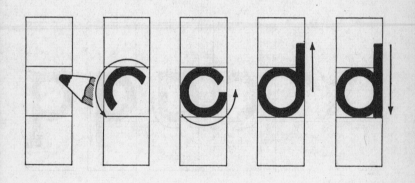

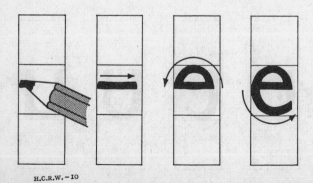

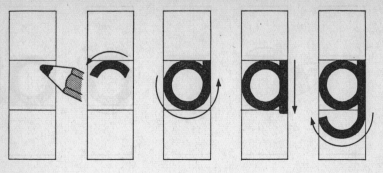

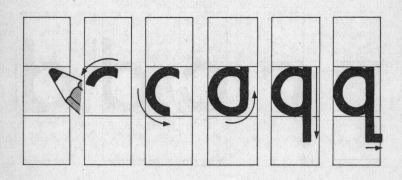

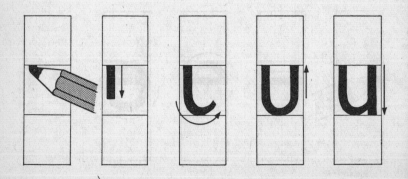

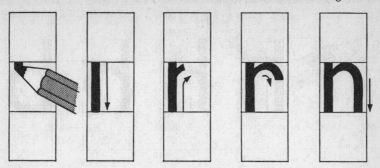

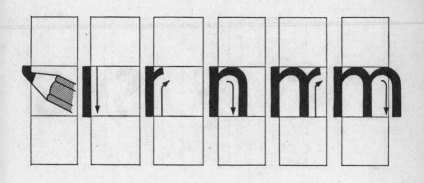

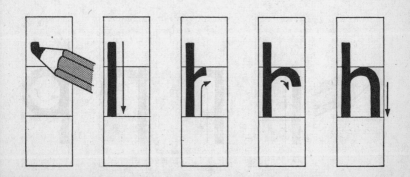

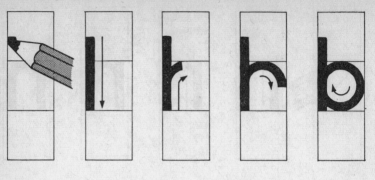

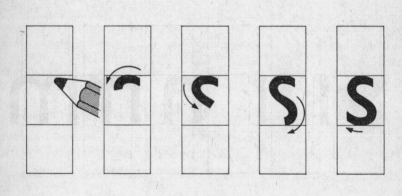

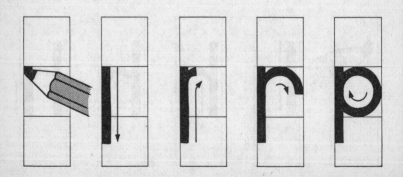

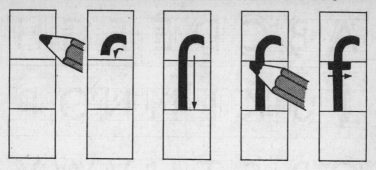

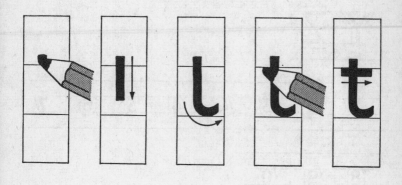

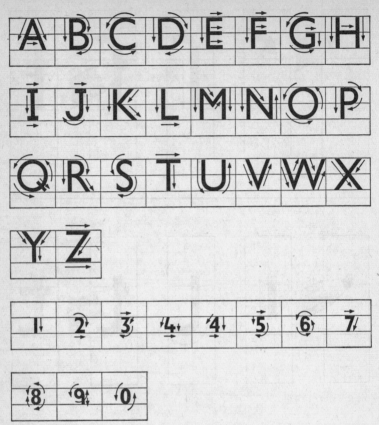

This is the information children need first to memorize. A little later they must also have information about the position the letter must be given in relation to the writing line (whether this is drawn in or not).

The drawings on pages 177–85 show the range of decisions the writer of a script must take. It is clearly not possible for children to master these without guidance and practice. If both are given to children once they need them, and are given regularly, patiently and with a purpose that goes beyond mere handwriting exercises, there is no reason why almost all children should not develop clear fluent handwriting fairly quickly and comfortably.

It is wrong to think that a child should be left to work out for himself the complex finger and wrist movements which form the basis of handwriting. Like spelling, handwriting is a skill which needs to become automatic, so that he is free to think about his message. If he is constantly thrown into doubt about how to make letter-shapes or how to order letter-shapes in words, his mind will be filled with uncertainty and uneasiness. His message will become distorted and lost sight of and he will become a reluctant writer.

Very young children will make their own attempts at the making of handwritten letters. At this stage they are very open to change and they will abandon awkward movements for more comfortable movements if these are shown to bring better results. But they must be allowed to make mistakes, especially those which happen because they have not quite reached the ability to do what is expected of them. They need the experience of making mistakes in order to remove the mistakes.

Children, like adults, vary in how they will eventually write and not all of them will become excellent calligraphers. So long as a handwritten text can be read without puzzlement, the writer has fulfilled his obligations to his readers and most children can easily learn writing good enough for the humble, everyday uses to which it is put, without the hours of handwriting practice which were once a compulsory part of the school day. We are not making handwriting machines, but helping people to present their thoughts on paper in clear, unpretentious ways.

The examples of children's work which follow have been chosen to show how progress was made in one particular classroom. Each piece of work chosen is typical of many children's handwriting performance. In every case, the emphasis is placed on the message, not on how it is produced. Yet this is not neglected. In the course of about a year, all children are seen to have had careful and thoughtful help with everything they need to know. The mark of successful learning is gradual mastery of the skill: a child begins haltingly because his task is immensely complex, bit by bit he builds up stamina, he writes more, he writes more clearly, more fluently and more quickly. This is important, for even at his fastest, there is a considerable difference between the speeds at which a writer is able to think silently and at which he can capture his thoughts and put them down on paper. He has greater need for fast, fluent writing than for rather slow, niggling neatness.

Examples of Children's Handwriting

Five-year-old boy:

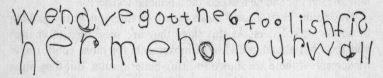

we have got the 6 foolish fishermen on our wall

The initial difficulty in reading this child's writing arises from two sources: omission of word spaces, and variations in the proportions of letter-shapes. The absence of a top margin has forced letter h to be written 'n'. As an afterthought the writer has revised his first draft by adding ascenders to his n shapes, irrespective of whether they represent n or h. The letter s in 'fishermen' is a reversal of the conventional letter shape. This is not a serious matter and will eventually be put right – especially when the shape of this letter is discussed and the way to make it is practised.

Five-year-old boy:

the car is a wrecked car it is on the dumped

The writing shows a clear understanding of word spaces. There are two errors which arise because of the way the sentence in this boy's head raced ahead of his writing. He checks back a little way to see what word he has reached and sometimes comes to the wrong conclusion. He has a problem with the beginning of his second sentence. He makes the final word of his first sentence do duty as the first word of his new sentence. In his mind he has several sentences related to his written text and these got slightly muddled:

the car is a wrecked car
the car is on the dump
the car was dumped

Five-year-old girl:

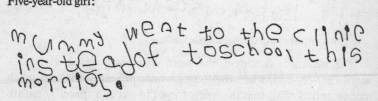

mummy went to the clinic instead of to school this morning.

A good example of writing which shows the problem a child may have in controlling all the features of handwriting throughout a text: letter-shapes are beginning to be made well but there is still some uncertainty. The proportions of letter e are consistently too large, as though e were considered especially important; e and c are not clearly differentiated and d, u and a are still difficult for this child to write. She fails completely with g.

The writing line has a typical wavy contour. Word spaces and line spaces are not used consistently. Easier to read than the first example however.

The same five-year-old, one month later:

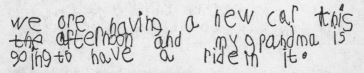

we are having a new car this afternoon and my grandma is going to have a ride in it.

The writing now shows considerably more control. Letter g has been mastered; word spaces are well used. Space between writing lines, the proportions of letter-shapes and their positions within the writing space still need mastering.

Five-year-old boy:

o a h you see the light
the lighthouseflashing. in

can you see the light in the lighthouse flashing

The writing is confident and word spaces are well controlled – until the very end, when the longer words probably took so much concentrated effort that the writer forgot to put in a space. There are however errors in n and c: the word 'can' is written u a h. Letters u and a have tails which will have to be shortened to the appropriate length. The writing line waves gently, and the positions of some letters (e.g. 'you', 'see', '-ght of light,' '-ing of flashing') show that the paper moved while the writing took place. It must be remembered that at this stage, handwriting is still a slow business and between the first letter and the last, a good deal of stopping and starting may take place. However, this boy has the beginnings of a very clear hand.

Five-year-old boy:

23 janua, ry

my brother. is playg at Rugby
and when he comes house I am
gog to box him.

my brother is playg at rugby and whan he comes house I am gog to box him (my brother is playing at rugby and when he comes home I am going to box him).

The writer has two problems unconnected with handwriting: he uses g to represent '-ing' ('playg' for playing and 'gog' for going), and the substitution of 'house' for 'home'. Otherwise his handwriting is coming along well. It has a wavy appearance but word spaces are well controlled. The consistent proportioning of letters is not yet seen to be important.

Five-year-old girl:

Yesterday I red my book I red it all the way through my self do you no what it is called? it is called LITTLE OLEO

The control of handwriting features is developing well. Word spaces are consistent, the proportion of letter sizes is most satisfactory, the writing waves a bit in the middle of the page but otherwise the writing lines are nicely horizontal.

Words like 'red'/'read' and 'no'/'know' are easily confused by children concerned to get down on paper the thoughts which pass very quickly through their heads. Words like 'yesterday', 'through', 'called' and 'little' are written correctly so that there is little reason to worry about this little girl. Afterwards the teacher talked about words which sound the same but which are written differently. 'Why?' asked the child. 'Because they don't mean the same.' She did not have to answer the further question: 'Then why don't we say them differently?' but she might have answered: 'In writing we do things that we don't do when we speak. With "red" and "read" try to write them so that there won't be any confusion between the colour and the act of reading.' We don't do anything about the difference between 'read' (present tense) and 'read' (past tense) because it is more important to give the reader the meaning (something to do with read) than to indicate the sounds in the spoken word red, (something to do with the colour red). It is not possible to change 'read' with '-ed' so we leave it alone.

Six-year-old boy:

9th June
I I was reading the pepere
tres moning and it sed
tere was a thunderstorm
and it stpouck a train
and mejd som rholes in it
and it hapend at Bolton.

I was reading the paper this morning and it said there was a thunderstorm and it struck a train and made some holes in it and it happened at Bolton.

A confident piece of writing in which many handwriting problems are still evident. None, however, interferes with the ideas the writer wishes to communicate. The teacher discussed certain spelling problems with the child and showed him how his words differed from the conventional spelling: 'pepere' – paper; 'thes' – this; 'moning' – morning; 'sed' – said; and so on. She very properly commented on how sensible most of his spellings were.

Six-year-old girl:

1st May

on Wednesday I went to
the dentist to have two teeth
out and I had to have a
tablet to make me go to
sleep so that I couldn't
feel anything at all and I
slept all the way home
with my city clothes on. DADDY put me in bed

A piece of writing with splendid control over all the major features of handwriting and spelling. It is important to note how difficult it is to hold a continuous stretch of language in one's mind while representing it faithfully in rather slow handwriting. This child has succeeded in this task and has obviously arrived at successful strategies for solving her spelling problems.

Six-year-old girl:

on the 9th of June it was my Dads Birthday. we
bought him two cards and a pen and a thermometer.
he was very satisfiet my Dad seb thank you. there
where things. the thermometer
was yellow and it showb maximum and
minimum. maximum was the hrerst and
minimam wa the shorirst.

Here is a very typical piece of 'news' with an interesting comment about Dad's reaction to his presents. The writer has obvious pleasure in using the words maximum and minimum, and also shows some indication of their meanings. The handwriting is gaining regularity and is well controlled. Much incidental teaching helped the child to reach this stage, but never more than the child was able to benefit from. With continuous help from her teacher the writer here will soon master the skill of handwriting. What she writes about and how she uses the language are more important problems which will take longer to learn. The teacher will still suggest handwriting practice but it will have a secondary place to any consideration of the quality of the child's written language.

Six-year-old boy:

April 18th

I am going to a party. Andrew will go to the swimming-bath with someone I know he is called philip. I have not done. the invitation. yes said my daddy to me you have not done the invitation. I am going to do it when I get home

This little boy has a clear idea of what a page should look like. He has mastered almost all the problems and has only to refine what he already knows about handwriting. He writes natural sentences, very much as he would speak them.

17 Alphabet and Speech-Sounds

Everyone knows that the alphabet exists – even children who do not know all the letters know that there *is* an alphabet. When speech-sounds are discussed, most children and many adults think of the alphabet and the sounds associated with the letters a to z. These are thought to sum up the speech-sounds of English speakers.

This is not so of course and the fault lies with the alphabet as well as with traditional teaching: with the alphabet because it has too few letters for all the speech-sounds it must represent; with traditional teaching because this has failed to clarify just how many speech-sounds there are and the ways in which the alphabet copes with this. Further, the pronunciation of our words is continuously but slowly changing and so the sounds that letters correspond to also change.

The question: What and how many speech-sounds are there? has many answers – as many answers as there are accents and speakers of English. Every speaker has an accent; accents differ because the set of speech-sounds of which they are made up, differ in some respects. This may mean that one speaker has fewer speech-sounds than another. It may also mean that speakers of different accents have the same number of speech-sounds without these being identical – but the differences between speakers are less than what they have in common.

To answer this question one has to select one accent as a model, the speech-sounds of which can then be listed. Since there is no universal set of English speech-sounds, this means that speakers with other accents have to adjust the list of speech-sounds to make it fit their own accent.

It is usual for the chosen accent to be that of southern British speakers who have what is sometimes called a B.B.C. accent. This is probably the most publicly used accent. It is also a well-regarded accent (for some speakers a 'posh' accent). We have therefore chosen this accent and list its speech-sounds.

The Speech-Sounds of One English Accent

Traditionally speech-sounds are divided into two groups:

(1) those speech-sounds which are made by restricting in some way the passage of air expelled from the chest. These are the consonants.
(2) those speech-sounds which are made by permitting the free passage of air expelled from the chest. Those are the vowels.

THE CONSONANTS

The consonant sounds are dealt with first and those which are represented by single letters will be listed first:

Speech-sound	*Corresponding Letter*
b as in **b**at	b
k as in **c**at	c, k, q, (x)
d as in **d**ad	d
f as in **f**at	f
g as in **g**irl	g
h as in **h**at	h
j as in **j**am	j, g
l as in **l**ad	l
m as in **m**um	m
n as in **n**et	n
p as in **p**at	p
r as in **r**at	r
s as in **s**at	s
t as in **t**ap	t
v as in **v**et	v
w as in **w**et	w
y as in **y**et	y
z as in **z**ip	z, s

This gives a total of eighteen speech-sounds, represented by twenty-two letters not including x (= ks). But this is only the total of speech-sounds represented by *single* letters. We also have:

sh as in **sh**ip represented by letters sh (also by ssi as in 'mission',
                       ti as in 'nation')

ch as in **ch**ip letter ch

th as in **th**in letters th

th as in **th**en letters th

ng as in si**ng** letters ng (nk)

zh as in vi**si**on letters si (as in 'vision', also su as in
            'measure', ge as in 'rouge').

The final total is twenty-four consonant speech-sounds.

In order for the alphabet to provide representations of these, five sets of two letters have to be added. In the case of the **zh** sound in 'vision', 'measure' and 'rouge', for instance, several combinations are used. As this is the rarest speech-sound, it does not need to be introduced to children until they are well advanced as readers and writers.

Though the alphabet dominates the awareness most people have of speech-sounds, alphabetical order which mixes consonants and sounds will not be used here. For the specialist student of speech-sounds a quite different order is necessary and one which has nothing to do with the alphabet. This new order carries several pieces of information for instance:

(1) Pairs of sounds which differ only because one of them is made with the vocal cords in their silent position. These pairs are called *voiced* sounds (with vocal cords vibrating) **z** in 'zip' and 'fizz', for example, and *voiceless* sounds (with vocal cords relaxed and silent) **s** in 'sit' and 'miss', for example.

(2) the parts of the vocal organs which participate in making the speech-sound. Thus the sounds **m** and **b** involve the lips while **f** and **v** involve top teeth and bottom lip. Speech-sound **h** (as in **h**ot) comes from far back in the mouth.

THE VOWELS

The vowel sounds of English are much more difficult to discover from the letters of the alphabet. There are five traditional vowel letters a, e, i, o, u. Their *names* (ay, ee, ie, oh, yoo) give one set of vowel sounds which these letters represent. These are, for a curious reason, referred to as the 'long' sounds. The same letters are used for what most people call the 'short' sounds. (Both 'long' and 'short' are quite inaccurate in describing the sounds.) Examples of words with long and short vowels are:

'short':	hat	met	bit	not	cut
'long':	hate	mete	bite	note	cute

The five traditional letters associated with vowel sounds omit one letter which has the dual function of representing a consonant *and* a vowel. Letter y is a consonant in the word 'yellow' and a vowel in words like 'cycle'. Like a, e, i, o, u, letter y represents two vowel sounds: 'short' as in 'baby'; 'long' as in 'my'.

Thus, the five letters a, e, i, o, u (letter y being a substitute for letter i in certain circumstances), give representations for ten vowel sounds:

Speech-Sound	Corresponding Letter
a as in 'cat'	a
ay as in 'Kate'	a+final e
e as in 'met'	e
ee as in 'mete'	e+final e
i as in 'bit'	i
ie as in 'bite'	i+final e
o as in 'not'	o
long **o** as in 'note'	o+final e
u as in 'cut'	u
long **u** as in 'cute'	u+final e

But ten vowel sounds is a long way short of our total. Here the insight afforded by the alphabet is much poorer than for consonant sounds. The belief that there are five vowel sounds (as opposed to five vowel letters) in English arises from the fact that people think about speech-sounds (of which they have little detailed awareness) in terms of letters (of which they are acutely aware through writing). Thus there is an underdeveloped aural awareness of speech-sounds in most literate adults, side by side with a well-developed visual awareness of letters.

THE 'MISSING' SOUNDS AND THEIR LETTERS

The English accent we are considering has twelve vowels which are single sounds. Only six have been noted ('cat', 'met', 'bit', 'not', 'cut', and 'teach'). Four of the remaining six are:

Speech-Sound	Corresponding Letters
ah as in 'father', 'car'	a and ar
short **oo** as in 'book'	oo
long **oo** as in 'food'	
long **aw** as in 'law'	aw and au

The two remaining single sounds in the vowel list are related sounds. They are not, however, associated with particular letters; there are several spelling representations of each and so our written words 'obscure' these vowels; they can be called obscured vowels.

The first is a long vowel sound found in syllables with strong or moderate stress. Some examples of it are: 'bird', 'girl', 'her', 'earth', 'fur', 'turn', 'church', 'word', 'journey' and 'colonel'.

The second is a very short vowel sound which occurs only in weakly stressed syllables. This vowel sound is even more 'obscured' by the variety of spellings which represent it. Indeed it is spelt with most vowel letters and combinations of letters. Here are a few of the many examples of this short obscured vowel which is sometimes called **schwa**:

(1) Letter **a** in 'drink**a** pint**a** milk**a** day' represents this vowel sound. The vowel sound of many words like 'a' and 'of' is **schwa** when these words receive weak stress (as they frequently do in normal speech). Other words of this kind (the *grammatical* words) are: 'the', 'to', 'for', 'have', 'had', 'shall', 'them', 'could'. All are normally pronounced with a short **schwa**. (So also is g.uh – the sound so often given corresponding to letter g: the **uh** is an attempt to spell the short **schwa**.)

Alphabet and Speech-Sounds 201

(2) In words like 'mother', the final vowel sound is short **schwa**: 'woman', 'gentlemen', 'waiter', 'doctor', 'china', 'colour', 'second', 'measure', 'human', 'breakfast', 'husband', 'moment', 'England', 'nonsense'.

(3) In words like 'about', the initial vowel sound is **schwa**: 'about', 'ago', 'alive', 'banana', 'parade', and in words such as: 'pronounce', 'gorilla', 'obey', 'police', 'tobacco', 'forget', 'potato'.

(4) **schwa** is also found in the middle of words such as: 'alphabet', 'comfortable', 'melody', 'decorate', 'Saturday', 'nobody'.

We shall use two examples from the above lists to represent the 'long' and 'short' obscured vowels: 'long' – 'girl'

'short' – 'mother'

Thus far, we have listed twelve single-sound vowels:

1 **a** in 'cat'
2 **e** in 'met'
3 **ee** in 'meet' (teeth)
4 **i** in 'bit'
5 **o** in 'not' (short aw)
6 **u** in 'cut'
7 **ah** in 'father'
8 short **oo** in 'book'
9 long **oo** in 'food'
10 long **aw** in 'law'
11 long **schwa** in 'girl'
12 short **schwa** in 'mother'

We have also listed three vowel sounds which are *diphthongs*, that is, each is made by gliding from one sound to another. There are five of these sounds:

13 the so-called long **a**, as in 'make'
14 the so-called long **i**, as in 'mine'   already listed on p. 199
15 the so-called long **o**, as in 'most'
16 the **ow**, as in 'cow'
17 the **oi**, as in 'boy'

This brings our total to seventeen vowel sounds.

The last three are also glides, but they all have one feature in common: each is a glide from one vowel sound to short **schwa**:

18 glide from **ee** to **schwa,** as in 'd**ear**'
19 glide from **e** to **schwa,** as in '**air**'
20 glide from **oo** to **schwa,** as in '**poor**'.

Notice that in the pronunciation of words like 'cute', 'pure', 'new', 'use' there is a consonant sound which is not written when spelling these words. Of the four speech sounds which make up 'cute' the second is the consonant sound we hear at the beginning of 'yes'. We could represent it like this 'k-y-oo-t'. In some accents this consonant is not present. Some New-Yorkers say 'noo' for 'nyoo'. In words like 'use' (this is no 'use') and 'use' ('don't use too much'), were the y consonant not present, the words would be 'oos' not 'yoos', and 'ooz' not 'yooz'. The spoken name of letter u – 'yoo' – begins with this consonant sound.

It surprises many speakers, especially those who have been led to think of the 'alphabet vowels' as the total for the language that there are in fact twenty vowels, not five. In this way a limited *awareness* of this aspect of their language is at variance with what they do – but do not know they do – especially when reading and writing. This is also one of the reasons why spelling is so badly taught. Teachers generally share this lack of awareness of how speech sounds are represented in written language.

Learning to spell, to be able to give the conventionally acceptable sequence of letters in a word, is something that children accept very early. The variety of spellings which children use in their early writing is necessary to their future development as writers. It is inevitable for them to begin with an oversimplified view of the way English spelling works. Their application of this simple view (one letter stands for one sound) will produce some right and some wrong answers. The growth of their knowledge of spelling can only continue if the simple one-letter-one-sound idea is radically altered by the addition of information which they must master step by step.

NOTES ON CONSONANT LETTERS

This means, for instance, that:

(1) the speech-sound **k** in 'cat' must be associated with letter c in 'cat', k in 'king', letters ck in 'back', q in 'queen', ch in 'school' and x in 'box' (where x = ks),

(2) the speech-sound **s** in 'sit' must be associated with letter s in 'sit', letter c in 'city',

(3) the speech-sound **j** in 'jam' must be associated with letter j in 'jam', letter g in 'gentle', letters dg in 'edge',

(4) the speech-sound **z** in 'zoo' must be associated with letter z in 'zoo' and letter s in 'his',

(5) the speech-sound **t** in 'tin' must be associated with letter t in 'tin' and with letters ed in 'wished'.

A list of consonant letters and their correspondences will be found on pages 197–8.

English words frequently cluster consonants together at the beginning and the end of syllables. These can cause problems for children.

Consonant clusters at the beginning of syllables			Consonant clusters at the end of syllables		
with l	with r	with s[1]	with l	with r	with s
blue	bright	scout	milk	arch	ask
cloth	cross	school	held	hard	wasp
flower	dry	skip	elf	forth	fast
glass	friend	slow	help	bark	
play	grow	smile	built	turn	
	pretty	snow		sharp	
	shrink	stop		start	
	three				
with w	with s[2]		with m	with n	with th
dwell	scribble		lamp	inch	width
swing	squash			hand	fifth
twin	splash			strange	warmth
	spring			thank	seventh
	string				length

-s endings have three pronunciations:

(1) **s** as in 'books'
(2) **z** as in 'trains'
(3) **iz** as in 'wishes'

-ed endings have three pronunciations:

(1) **t** as in 'wished'
(2) **d** as in 'huffed'
(3) **id** as in 'mended'

In words like 'thumb', the final consonant letter **b** is traditionally known as a 'silent' letter. This is not a helpful term. All letters are silent, as we have pointed out. As **b** following **m** is never pronounced in single-syllable words we have to explain that the **b** is written but not spoken. Children should have the opportunity to compare 'thum' and 'thumb' so that they can *see* the difference between what represents the speech sounds of 'thum' and its spelling equivalent. In this case, **mb** may be taken as another way of writing **m**. However, in a word like 'number' the m is in the first syllable ('num') and the b is the in second ('ber'), and so both are pronounced.

Note that in the following words similar problems occur:

'reign'	:	gn	is pronounced	**n**
'know'	:	kn	,,	,,	**n**
'talk'	:	lk	,,	,,	**k**
'salmon'	:	lm	,,	,,	**m**
'half'	:	lf	,,	,,	**f**
'lamb'	:	mb	,,	,,	**m**
'autumn'	:	mn	,,	,,	**m**
'listen'	:	st	,,	,,	**s**
'often'	:	ft	,,	,,	**f**
'write'	:	wr	,,	,,	**r**
'sword'	:	sw	,,	,,	**s**
'island'	:	is	,,	,,	**ie**
'honest'	:	h	is not pronounced

NOTES ON VOWEL LETTERS

The values of vowel letters vary much more than those of consonant letters. Vowel sounds also vary from accent to accent and because of this each speaker has to discover the equivalent values for letters in his accent to those described here. There is not and cannot be a universal set of values for letters. This is particularly true of the vowel sounds and vowel letters.

In English spelling vowel letters have a marked variety of values. This is true in two ways:

(1) Some *vowel sounds* are represented by several different letters. For instance the short **aw** sound of the word 'hot' is written as:

   o in 'hot'
   a in 'what'
  ou in 'cough'
  ow in 'knowledge'
  au in 'because'

(2) Some *vowel letters* represent several different vowel sounds. Again, take vowel letter **o** as in 'hot'. We write o in each of the following words:

'hot':	o	represents short **aw**
'one':	o	represents **wu**
'old':	o	represents o ('long' o)
'son':	o	represents o ('short' u)
'of':	o	frequently represents short **schwa** (ugh)
'do':	o	represents oo
'so':	o	represents oh ('long' o)
'gone':	o-e	represents short **aw** (as in 'hot')
'home':	o-e	represents oh ('long' o)

Certainly not all letters and sounds are related in such a variety of ways as this, but there are enough examples to suggest strongly that children should be helped to think of vowel letters and vowel sounds as being related to each other in different ways and not just in the first way they are told. The one-letter : one-sound notion is a deception. While it persists in a child's mind unaltered, it will cause endless difficulties.

English spelling is, as we have seen, full of inconsistencies and ambiguities. Many systems have been devised in attempts to make reading easier for the beginner. In some, for instance *i t a* (*initial teaching alphabet*) extra letters are added to the alphabet. Other methods retain the conventional alphabet helping the reader to grasp the different sound values of the same letter, or visual symbol, by marking letters with accents (diacritics) or by colours.

The *Diacritical Marking System* (DMS) was devised by Edward Fry, an American. In this system most consonants and 'short' vowels are not marked in any way. 'Long' vowels have a bar over them: 'gō', 'hē'; **schwa** has a comma over it: 'ȧbove'; silent letters are crossed out: 'lamb̸'; two-letter symbols like sh have a bar placed under them: '**sh**'; alternative values for c, g have a bar placed under them: ç̱ellar, g̱em.

Words in Colour by Dr Caleb Gattegno was introduced to schools in Britain in 1962. In this system colour is used to distinguish different pronunciations of the same letter or the same pronunciation of different letters. Thus **t** is mauve, **a** is white, **p** is brown, etc.

Colour Story Reading by Kenneth Jones uses four colours red, blue, green, black, and a square, circle and triangle as background shapes, each of which may be red, blue or green. In this system the words 'do', 'two', 'woo', 'drew', 'true', 'shoe' and 'through' have the green circle drawn round the letters which represent the '**oo**' sound. The author also provides stories which help children to form a network of associations in which colours, shapes and sounds are linked by the story imagery. This idea is not new, but it has seldom been presented so thoroughly as here.

These and other systems of reading methods are described and discussed in detail in a survey of methods and devices for teaching reading: Pat D'Arcy, *Reading for Meaning. The Report of a Survey carried out for the Schools Council. Volume 1: Learning to Read,* Hutchinson Educational for the Schools Council, London, 1973.

In another book, *Success and Failure in Learning to Read,* Penguin Books, Harmondsworth, 1973, Ronald Morris discusses the early stages of learning to read in a sympathetic and critical way. He also examines how some readers reach their 'reading maturity' and others become backward. Although written for teachers, parents will find much of interest to them in this fine book.

Vowel Letters and Spelling Patterns

Because the simple vowel letters a, e, i, o, u, and y have alternative values ('mat', 'mate') these values have to be signalled visually. This is done in one of several ways:

'bit'
 〉 'short' **i**   One consonant letter following the vowel letter in single-syllable words signals 'short' value. In
'bitten'
words of more than one syllable, the consonant must be doubled – or there must be two different consonants (e.g. 'resting') for the 'short' value to be selected.

'bite'
 〉 'long' **ie**   Final consonant followed by e in single-syllable words, signals the 'long' value. In words of more
'biting'
than one syllable, the final e is no longer needed because one consonant letter following the vowel letter now signals the 'long' value.

This change in signalling is regularly seen in the way the addition of '-ing' affects certain single-syllable verbs. There are three possibilities here:

(1) (a) 'paint' becomes 'painting': no change.

    (b) 'make' becomes 'making': the final e is deleted before -ing is added.

In 'making' (mak+ing) a single consonant k follows the single vowel letter 'a', the value of which is **ay**.

    (c) 'run' becomes 'running': the final consonant n is doubled.

In 'running' (runn+ing) the doubled consonant **nn** which follows the single vowel letter **u**, signals the choice of the 'short' value for **u** (as in 'cup').

(2) In the words 'give', 'live' and 'have' the final e does not signal a 'long' vowel value. It is, however, obligatory because in English spelling letter v is never permitted to end a word. Recent additions to the language such as 'Rev', 'gov', 'lav', 'rev' (up) and 'spiv' are all contractions and from being separated initial syllables have been accepted as words. Letter v is seldom doubled (but e.g.: 'navy', 'navvy'). In 'giv+ing', 'liv+ing', 'hav+ing', letters i and a have their 'short' value.

(3) Words ending in le have similar 'short' and 'long' consonant signals:

'short'	*'long'*
paddle (padd+le)	**a**ble (ab+le)
little (litt+le)	bible (bib+le)
bubble (bubb+le)	bugle (bug+le)

Spelling in words with single vowel letters can be summarized thus: in single syllable words, one consonant following the vowel letter signals 'short' value; the 'long' value requires a final e. In two-syllable words one consonant following the vowel letter signals 'long' value; and two different consonants or doubled consonants signal 'short' value. So in single-syllable words and two-syllable words apparently similar signals have to be given different interpretations.

There are some more 'long' values for simple vowels:

(1) In two letter words e, o and y are 'long':
   be, he, me, we (also she)
   go, no, so
   by, my
   she, where **sh** though two letters, is one visual symbol.

(2) In most, post, ghost, host, the o represents the 'long' **oh**.
   In child, wild, find, behind, kind, mind, rind, bind the i represents the 'long' **ie**.

There are special values for letters **o**, u and a:

(1) Letter o has the value 'short' **u** (as in 'up'):

come	done	among	dove	colour
some	money	tongue	glove	dozen
	monday	monkey	love	
	month	(but not	oven	
	none	donkey)	onion	
	son		shove	
	won			

(2) Letter o has the value **oo**:

do ⎱ only when strongly   move   woman   tomb
to ⎰ stressed   lose   wolf   womb
two   prove
who
whose
whom

(3) Letter u has the value **oo**:

bull	bush	put	Ruth	sugar
full	push	pudding	truth	sure
pull	puss			cuckoo

(4) Special values for letters a and o:

a as long **aw**:   o as long **o**:
 ball   roll (but not doll)
 halt   stroll

a as short **o**:   a as long **aw**
 want   wasn't   warm
 wash   watch   water
 was   what

There are special representations of 'short' i. In words which have a weak stress on one syllable, no matter whether the letter a or e is written, it is pronounced as 'short' **i**:

a written	e written
cabbage	eleven
village	elephant
palace	because
	enjoy
	chicken
	women

> kitchen
> biggest
> forest
> pocket

Complex vowel symbols (those made up of two letters) are listed here. Under each two-letter symbol, any important variations in the value of the symbol are given:

(1) ai as in 'rain' and ay as in 'day'.
   Also: said (sed)
          again (-gen)
          against (-genst)
(2) aw as in 'paw' and au as in 'sauce'.
   Also: aunt
          laugh
(3) ea as in 'sea'.
   Also: bread   great
          head   break
                   steak
(4) ee as in 'tree'.
   Also: been (bin).
(5) ey as in 'they' and ei as in 'reindeer'.
   Also: eye   ceiling   leisure
          key   receive
                 receipt
                 seize
(6) ew as in 'few' (fyoo), 'grew' (groo), and eu as in 'Europe'.
   Also: sew
(7) ie as in 'die' and ye as in 'dye'.
   Also: movie   friend
          field
(8) oa as in 'road',
   Also: abroad
(9) oo as in 'book' and 'food'.
   Also: blood
          flood
(10) ou as in 'house'.
   Also: soul

        young
        group

(11) ow as in 'cow'.

   Also: know

There are special spellings of vowel letters with letter r:

ar	er	ir	or	ur
arm	her	bird	storm	fur
are	**ere**	**ire**	**ore**	**ure**
care	here	fire	store	cure
air	**ear**	**eir**	**oar**	**our**
fair	hear	their	roar	flour
Also:			Also:	
bear			pour	journey
learn			your	courage
			four	

eer	ier	oor
beer	pier	poor

(12) The famous -gh words and their exotic pronunciations

-ough words

ough = aw as in 'law'

ought

bought

thought

sought

fought

wrought

ough = ow as in 'how'

plough

bough

drought

ough = 'long' o as in 'go'

dough

though

ough = oo as in 'food'

through

ough = schwa as in 'mother'

thorough

borough

ough='short' o + f as in 'off'

cough

trough

ough='short' u+f as in 'puff'

rough

enough

tough

-augh words

augh=aw as in 'law'

caught

taught

daughter

naughty

augh='long' ah as in 'rather'+f

laugh

draught

-eigh words

eigh='long' a as in 'made'

neigh

weigh

freight

weight

eight

neighbour

sleigh

eigh='long' i as in 'mine'

height

-aigh words

aigh='long' a as in 'made'

straight

By comparison the following gh words are a dull lot:

high	bright	ghost	spaghetti	yoghourt
sigh	fight	ghastly		
thigh	knight	ghetto		
	light			
	might			
	night			

19 Some Conclusions Concerning Reading, Writing and Spelling

Many of the books mentioned on pages 80–99 – read and re-read as often as children request – will support reading and also extend and enhance the reader's personal experience, making available to him different kinds of knowledge. In all work of this kind the teachers' concern should be that children respond to the experiences that books provide in a way which enriches their inner world. Learning about speech-sounds, letters and word recognition are interests children readily take up if reading and writing are already activities in which they enjoy participating in their own ways.

As Patrick clearly demonstrated, the child's approach to spelling must begin with an understanding of the underlying principles of spelling and writing. The shapes of the letters, the letter names, the ability to relate letters to sounds are all being mastered by Patrick. His spelling 'mistakes' can all be explained to him because the principle on which he is working is clear. He lacks information about spelling but then this is so for every beginner. There is no harm in using information wrongly as long as there is access to missing information. This may come haphazardly from reading from noticing words in the environment, from newspapers, comics and television. It may also come from direct teaching.

Spelling is not as easy to teach or to learn as some people think. English spelling is complex and sometimes wayward. It is not a confused jumble as some suggest. Much of it is highly and consistently patterned. Its mastery will be easier if the attention of children is chiefly given to the responses their reading affords them, to the illumination their reading brings them and not to the 'service skills' involved in learning to spell. This latter is more likely to move children when they have a growing interest in language. And this is something we all have unless bungled teaching and boring texts kill it.

Readers and Writers as Spellers

The act of reading aloud requires the reader to acknowledge written symbols and to fit these on to the structures of grammar and meaning he already has 'in his head'. It is, however, the *meaning* he is pursuing. Merely recognizing individual words will not provide the meaning that lies in a text – if he is unable to relate these to his own meanings and to uses of language he has experienced, he will have done little more than identify a list of words. To avoid this the beginner-reader needs plenty of experience of many texts which he can read for their meaning and respond to. If his response to a text is weak, something is wrong.

All the activity which we label reading is *silent*: the recognition of visual words, matching them to known words 'in the head' adding new words to this head list, identifying an unrecognized word by the application of letter-sound information, using clues from other words in the context and from pictures, building a sequence of grammatical and semantic structures and finally responding to the text as though to another speaker: all this is *silent* activity.

When young children begin to read, they very often accompany their silent reading by pronouncing what they have read. This is an *additional* activity to that of reading and one which therefore slows down the process. Two jobs take longer than one. Too great a demand for reading aloud – which still happens in the teaching of reading – may, in the end, force a reader to become slower than he need be. Children who learn to read early in their lives tend to take up reading for their own pleasure, because they cannot get enough by being read to, and they quickly learn to read without pronouncing what they read.

Reading, although it gives visual experience of words, does not by this token provide the information needed to spell. The reader may note the spelling of the words he reads but he is not reading primarily in order to find out how to spell, any more than when he listens to people talking he is finding out how to pronounce words. In each case it is the meaning which is paramount. Good readers may in fact be rather indifferent spellers, and if they have poor recall of certain sequences of letters they may continue all their lives to spell certain words in a personal rather than a conventional manner. The fluent reader is not recognizing words so much as word meanings. The long familiarity he has with words tends to make him very little aware of the act of word recognition. Familiarity in this case breeds expectation: what he expects the text to have, he will predict it has and so may read what is not there. It is for this reason that proof-reading is so difficult, particularly when a mistake involves a single letter in a word. The beginner-reader whose *visual* familiarity with words is slight, has to look at words much longer to identify them. However, with growing experience, he learns more than just the words he reads: he learns what to expect words to look like. He will learn this better if he is not hampered by a diet of three-letter words only, for that can only give him information about what three-letter words look like.

There is no doubt that, in the end, writing down the correct sequences of letters in written words is more taxing than reading words in which this has already been done. It is also more difficult to lay hold of one's thoughts and get them on to paper in a well-ordered cogent manner. It takes a great deal of practice. It is therefore the more surprising that children are able to do this so well while they are still very young and that in certain classrooms they enjoy doing so. Having something to write is like having something to say. And whenever there are responsive listeners and readers, there is no shortage of things to talk about and write about. It is the right kind of other people who make both possible.

20 A Story called *Roy the Boy*

In chapter 4 we discussed Patrick's story, *Roy the Boy*. It is a remarkable achievement for a five-and-a-half-year-old, with a long and complex narrative and a range of characters handled with confidence and competence. Some typical pages of the manuscript and a full transcript in the original spelling are reproduced below.

Roy the Boy: The Full Text

Page 1   – CHAPTER ONE – ONCE THER WAS A MAN HE WAS TERBLE BRAV WEN HE WAS GOING TO FLY IN ANN AIR-CRAFT HE WUD ALWAS CARY A PARSHOOT WITH HIM ONE DAY HE WENT TO THE AIROPLANE PLASE AND HE

Page 2   BURT A DO IT YOUR SELF AIROPLANE AND HE MADE IT HIMSELF AND WENE HE FINISHT IT HIS WIFE MARMELR WUD GO TO THE LISENS SHOP AND GER A LISENSE AFTER ALL OF THET

Page 3   – CHAPTER TWO – THE MAN LET HIS WIFE TEST IT TO SEE IF IT WOS BROKON WITCH IT WAS NOT AND AFTER THE TEST THEY HAD A LOVELEE TIME FLYING IN THE AIR.

Page 4   AND ON THE 13 TH OF MAY MARBELRE AND HIS FATHRE HAD A BABY NAMDE ROWY ROWY WOS VERY GOOD BABY AS SOON AS HE GOT HOME

Page 5   HE WENT TO SLEP HE WAS SO TIRD AND HE DID NOT HAVE A KOT TO SLEP IN WHEN ROWYS' MOTHER & FATHER RILISD THIS THEY WENT TO THE KOT SHOP AND BORT A KOT WENE THEY GOT HOME

Page 6   – CHAPTER THREE – THEY PUT THE SWET BABY IN HIS KOT IN THE MORNING IT WOS ROWY'S BIRTHDAY THEY WERE KAKES AND JELY AND JAMTARTS ROWY WAS SO PLESD HE JUMPT UP AND DOWN AND WENT DOM DE DUM DE ALL THE TIME.

Page 7   HE GOT PREANTS AND BAJIS AND BITHDAY CARDS THE NEKST

⑥

INT He MORNING
HE SAW HIS
DATIS AND
R4L ISD
THEY HE
WOS TWO
YIRS OWLD
HE WAS
TRILY PLESDE
DAWNST
UP AND
DAWN
THE SEKOND
TIME
HE TUMDT
UP HE
TUMDT
RITE OWT
OF HIS
KOT

DAY He GOT MORe PRESANTS AND EXSPESHLE A LOVeLE PILOSHET
TO PUT ON HIS PILO THeT NITe ROWY DREMPT OF PRESENTS AND
PILOSHETS

Page 8   IN THe MORNING He SAW HIS BAJIS AND RILISD THeT He WOS
TWO YIRS OWLD He WaS RILY PLESDe BAWNST UP AND DOWN
THe SEKOND TIMe He JUMPT UP He JUMPT RITe OWT OF HIS KOT.

Page 9   AFTER THeT IT WOS BREKFAST ROWY ET HIS BIFOR MARBELAR
AND HER FATHeR ON TUSeDAY IT WaS ROWY'S BIRTHDAY AGAN
AND IT WaS JUST THe SAME THING.

Page 10 ONe DAY ROWY WaS HAVING A LOVELY TIME FLYING INTHe AIR
WITH HIS MUM AND DAD THe BRAV MANS NAME WaS SUPER-
STRONG ONE DAY THeR HOUSe KORT FIRe!

Page 11 AND NOBODY NEWe! BUT SUPER STRONG DID He GOT HIS LADER
AND RESQD ROY BUT ROY'S MOTHeR ESKAPT HERSELF AND MET
SUPER STRONG AND

Page 12 ROWY IN THe GARDEN GETING WATER TO PUT OUT THe FIRe
THEN IN FIVe MINITSe THe FIRe WaS OUT THeN AFTER THeY
WENT TO THe

Page 13 CAPTER FORe – PLANe AND GOT THe MAP OF ENGGLEND AND
WENT ALL OVER LONDON TO FIND A PLASe TO LIVE IN BUT THeY
KUD NOT A PLASe LUKILY THeY HAD TWO CAMP BEDS AND TWO
SLEING BAGS WITH THeM AND THe KOT.

Page 14 IN THe MORING THeY WER SETING OF AGAN BUT THIS TIM JUST
AS THeY WERe TAKING OF A MAN SHAWTID DOWNT GO YOU
CAN LIVe WITH ME SO THeY STOPT AND ASKT IF THeY HAD A

Page 15 PLASe TO PUT THER AIROPLANe YES SEDe THe MAN THeR IS INUF
ROOM IN MY GARAGE FOR ONe MILIYON ANTS TO LIVe IN JUST
THEN THeY HAD ANOTHeR TEST BUT IT WUD NOT GO SO THe

Page 16 MAN WENT BACK TO HIS HOMe AND GOT SOMe ROPe AND HIS
CAR WEN He GOT BACK He TIDe ONe END OF THe ROPe TO THe
AIROPLAN AND OTHeR TO HIS CAR AND He TOWD THe PLANe
TO HIS GARAGe

Page 17 AFTTER THeT THe MAN BACKT HIS CAR INTO THe GARAGE AS
WELL BECAUSE THe PLANe WaS MENDID OF CORSe. IN THe
MORNING THeY WERe VERY PLESDe TO BEING SAVD

Page 18 SO THeY THANGKT THe Man AFTER ALL THIS THeY SET OF AGAN
THeY WERe STILL VERY PLESDe OF BEING AS ENYWY THeR CAR

Page 19 – CHAPTER 5 – WaS BLON UP ALLREDY IN THe FIRe ON THe

② CHAPTER SEVEN

IT WAS NOT,
ROY TOLD
MARBECAR
TO STOP
THE ~~AIRC~~
~~AIRCRAFT~~
AIRCRAFT A MINITE
SO THEY
HE COUDE
GET HIS
GUN.
TO PLAY
WITH
IN THE
~~PLACE~~
PLANE

18TH OF MAY AT LAST THEY FOWND A PLASE TO LIVE IN THEY LOOKT ALL ARAWND THE UNDENTIFID HOUSE.

Page 20 – CHAPTER SIX – AFTER THE EXPOISHON THEY UNPAKT THE MAP AND THE CAMP BEDS AND THE SLEPING BAGS AND THE KOT AFTER THEY WENT TO THE POLICE TO SEE IF THEY NEW THE FIRE AND IF THEY KUD LIVE IN THE

Page 21 HOUSE. MENWHILLE. IN THE MIDDEL OF THE NITE ROY WOKE UP THEN HE HERD A SOUD IT WENT LIKE THIS WOO HOO ROY THORTE IT WAS A GOST HE TREMBELD FOR A MOMENT THEN HE RINEMBERD

Page 22 HE WAS THREE YEERS OLD SO BIG BOYS OF THET AGE CODE NOT BE SKARD OF A GOST SO HE WENT BACK TO BED AND HAD A GOOD LONG SLEP FOR HE MIST BRAKFAST HIS MOTHER MARBELER HAD TO KISS

Page 23 HIM 20 TIMES TO WAKE HIM UP. IN THE MORNING ROWY HAD TO GO TO SCOOLL. FOR THE FIRRST TIME he WENT MARBELLAR HAD TO KUIME WITH HIM HE HAD TO LERN PRERS

Page 24 and EXSPESHALLY WORK TO DO ROY GOT HOME HE WENT TO HIS BED TO HAVE a SLEEP HE FOUND a TOY GUN IT WOS CALLD MARX M–16 ROY HAD a

Page 25 GREAT TIME PLAYING WITH HIS TOY GUN THEN HE GOT BORD and WONTID SOMETHING ELS TO DO. HE WENT OUT IN THE GARDEN a LOOK HOO HE SOR MARBELLAR and

Page 26 SUPER STRONG FLYING OUBUT IN THE AIRCRAFT THEY HAD BORT SUPER STRONG JUMPT OF and PIKT UP ROY and FLEW UP AUCAN IT WAS MUCH BETER THEN SHOOTING NOTHING ! INDED

Page 27 – CHAPTER SEVEN – IT WAS NOT. ROY TOLD MARBELAR TO STOP THE AIRCRAFT a MINITE SO THWT HE CUDE GET HIS GUN, TO PLAY WIT IT IN THE PLANE

Page 28 DONT WORY WIRE LANDING ROY

Page 29 ROY SEDE WEN IS MY BRIDYDAY AGEN FEPVERY SEDE SUPER STRONG ITS JANUARY. NOW ROY YEARS PASST BUT ROY WAS SAD HE HAD

Page 30 NO FREND at SCOL HE WAS SEVEN BY THE TIME HE HAD a FREND BEFORE HE HAD A FREND HIS MOTHEAR WAS PREGNANT AN had to GO TO HOSPETAL

Page 31 FOR ROYS BOY FREND. ON TUESDAY FROM WEPENSDAY ROY HAD

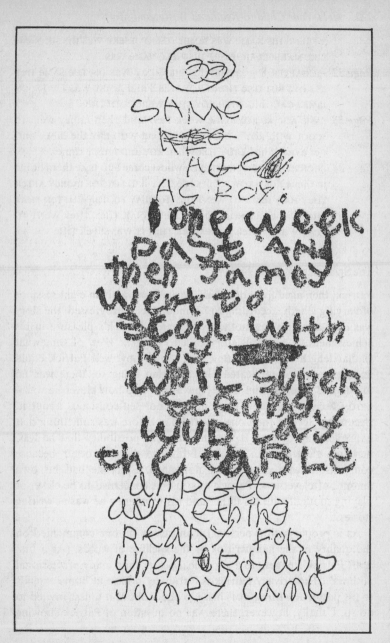

22

SAME
~~REG~~ AGE
AS ROY.

1 ore week
past an
then Jamey
went to
Seoul with
Roy
whil super
strong
wud lay
the table
and get
everthing
ready for
when Roy and
Jamey came

a FRENd HIS NAME WaS JaMEY JESERP JESERP WaS HIS SIR NAME LIKe MARBELLAR JESERP HIS RIELE NAME WaS

Page 32 – CHAPTER 8 – JaYMEY his BIRTHDaY WaS ON THE SAME DaY aS ROYS BUT ONE THING ROY WaS 8 and JaMEY WaS TWO SOON JaMEY CAUGhtC WITH ROY THEY WERE BOTH THE

Page 33 SAME AGE AS ROY. One WeeK PaST ANd Then Jamey Went to SCOOL WIth ROY WhiL SUPER StRONG WUD LaY the taBLe anD Get aVrething REaDY FOR When ROY anD Jamey camé

Page 34 BaCK at 4 0 0 P m marBeLLa whuM come anD take them home in theRe ROLS-ROWIYS BECOSE thay haD LOTS OF money AFTER THEY HAD TEa AND WeNT OUT TO PLAY FOOTBAW AFTER THAT THEY CAME IN AND HADE A LITELE SNAK THEN THEY WeNT TO PLAY WHITH THER TOYS AFTER THET IT WAS SUPER TIME

The Spelling of *Roy the Boy*

Patrick, then aged five and a half, wrote it privately in eight sessions of varying length, according to his mood. As it progressed, the story was read aloud to his mother who shared Patrick's pleasure in his achievement. A previous story called *Patsy out West* of somewhat similar length to *Roy the Boy*, had shown how well Patrick could manage a long complicated plot and that being so, there was no undue fuss made of him now. He was not told how clever he was – partly because he knew this and was not self-conscious about it. Becoming cleverer than one was the day before was something that happened day by day. It was normal. The possibility that he was, perhaps, cleverer than others of his age did not occur because comparisons with others were not made. Everyone had his own amount of cleverness. Patrick was just as concerned to be clever at playing football with his father and his brother as he was at writing stories.

As is proper with a personal manuscript, no one commented on the quality of the handwriting or the spelling of words. (As a first draft Patrick's pages are a good deal neater than many professional authors'.) The privacy Patrick is fortunate to have at home extends to his personal writing. It is his. No one looks at it unless invited to do so. Usually, however, there was no question of Patrick showing

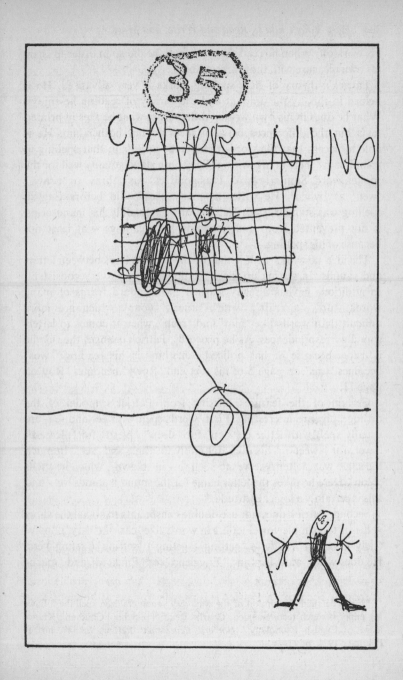

his work off. When he read the text aloud, he did so in order to share his own pleasure with those around him.

Patrick's theory of how spelling works is very advanced. He is helped in this by the amount and the variety of reading he enjoys. What he does in his own writing differs from what he sees in printed texts but the differences between them do not bother him. He is able to accept that the word 'there' may appear in that spelling in print but as 'ther' in his writing. They both stand equally well for the spoken word. Similarly 'wos' is as good as 'was', 'brav' as 'brave', 'wen' as 'when'. He writes as many people did before English spelling was standardized. He, and anyone reading his manuscript, is not prevented from understanding his meanings – at least not because of his spelling.

The idea he works with is that of the relationships between letters and sounds. In setting up these relationships he is very consistent. In addition, he has already learned the standard forms of many words: 'do', 'aircraft', 'wife', 'after', 'your', which are more difficult than words like 'him' and 'man', when it comes to letter-sound correspondences. As he proceeds, Patrick changes the rule he is using, because he has noticed something in his reading: 'wos' becomes 'was' on page 5 of his text and 'Rowy' becomes 'Roy'on page 11.

Certain of the features missing from Patrick's model of the orthography are interesting. First, words spelt with ee- and -ea- are usually spelt with letter e ('slep' for 'sleep', 'plesd' for 'pleased', 'swet' for 'sweet'). This does not apply to 'three and 'see'. In much the same way, letter o serves to spell -ow in 'blown', which he spells 'blon'. Here he takes the letter name for the sound it stands for – and this is certainly a logical attitude.*

Second, Patrick does not use double consonants to signal the short value of the simple vowel letters in words like 'carry' ('cary'), 'jelly' ('jely'), 'ladder' ('lader'), 'getting' ('geting'), 'setting' ('seting') etc. He does write 'ann' for 'an', 'Engglend' for 'England' and 'mean-

---

*For a detailed description of the way very young children spell the following paper is much recommended: Charles Read, 'Pre-School Children's Knowledge of English Phonology', *Harvard Educational Review*, vol. 41, no. 1, February 1971, pp. 1–34.

whille' for 'meanwhile', so that the idea of doubling is there, but its purpose is not clear to him.

Third, Patrick does not know about the use of c = /k/, ck = /k/ and c = /s/. Usually he writes k for the sound /k/ and s for the sound /s/. However, some words have already been learned and are spelt correctly – 'once', 'camp', 'craft'. Towards the end of the manuscript 'school' appears as 'scooll', 'could' as 'cude'. On page 17, 'back' is correctly spelt.

Some of Patrick's c/k/ck errors are:

letter s for letter c (soft)	letter k for letter c (hard)	letter k for letters ck
'plase' for 'place'	'kakes' for 'cakes'	'unpakt' for 'unpacked'
	'kort' for 'caught'	
	'eskapt' for 'escaped'	
	'kud' for 'could'	
	'kot' for 'cot'	
	'skard' for 'scared'	

The fourth and most important point is that Patrick does not know about the -ed past tense ending. He does not write letter z for the sound zed in words like 'his' ('hiz'), 'pleesed' 'pleezd'), 'was' ('woz') but writes them quite correctly with letter s. However, he writes the -ed ending as either -t or -d. He is working on the basic notion: 'I write the letter which stands for the sound I hear when I say the word'. Thus he writes 'jumpt' for 'jumped', 'savd' for 'saved' and 'mendid' for 'mended'. In this he is consistent, that is, he represents the three spoken past tense endings -t, -d and -id. He does not know that the orthography uses -ed for all three.

Patrick's treatment of the -ed ending is:

/t/ ending		/d/ ending		/id/ ending
eskapt	pickt	plesd	resqd	shawtid
stopt	passt	tide	towd	
askt	mist	trembld	skard	
unpakt				

In *Roy the Boy*, Patrick shows how he is discovering additional facts about letters and sounds on his own (or at least by his own efforts) without anyone but himself correcting his errors. Self-correction like this is indeed what all children have to achieve. Correction from outside will *not necessarily* make any difference at all to the learner unless it fits into what he knows about spelling. Patrick's spelling is steadily moving towards the conventional spelling set out in dictionaries.

This means that he is successfully modifying his ideas of how to spell without any difficulty. In this he is helped by two factors: the effect of regular reading and the help others give him whenever he asks for it. But most of the time he solves problems in spelling in his own way because he is concerned much more deeply with the ideas he is expressing on paper. This does not mean that concern for meaning is incompatible with learning to spell conventionally, provided the right influences are at work. If they are not, personal spellings may eventually be hard to change – especially as children grow older.

At school, the children in Patrick's class were asked to write a poem, a common enough activity in many contemporary classrooms. Patrick had heard a great many poems from his mother since he was a baby. He knew very well what poetry sounded like. What he did not know was what it looked like when written down. So when he responded to the invitation 'to write a poem' he did so with a clear idea of how it would sound when read aloud.

Now it is autumn

now it is autumn leaves are falling
softly so. no for summer it has
gone. the sun has shon its last
shine. while all the leaves are
piled in a line. in the vine
the grapes are starting while
the leaves and trees are part-
ing down down where the people
tread dive the leaves the dry ones
dead. Sleeping sleeping till there
burnt. gardeners come and go
away while on the ground the
leaves do lay. gardeners sweep
and burn the leaves. while
the people have wooly clothes.
the trees are bear and we
dont' care

He knows that poetry allows the writer to use language in a way that is special. Thus he writes 'the sun has shon its last shine', and rhymes 'shine' with 'line' and 'vine' and invents images to fit. Indeed he goes on rhyming his lines so inventively that one is full of admiration for the success he makes of this difficult technique. Seldom does it seem to force him to write away from the subject matter and the feeling of his 'poem'.

He uses literacy devices with typical relish: thus he writes 'softly so', not just 'softly' and immediately rhymes 'so' with 'no'. Then he inserts 'it' in 'for summer it has gone', so conveying a rhythmic finality and even a touch of melancholy. How readily English readers will be able to visualize the dull grey days he conjures up from the line 'the sun has shon its last shine' (a reversal as it were, of 'shine out, fair sun!'). And the pitifully small grapes just starting to grow on the outdoor London vine as the summer ends. Naive poetics such as these are no less delightful – and no less ephemeral – than the bold colours and compositions of children's paintings. In Patrick's verse-making, invention bubbles up like spring water, creating linguistic images out of his feelings and responses to experience and out of his new awareness of 'heightened' language.

Less than a year separates *Roy the Boy* and *Now it is autumn*. In that time Patrick extended the range of his prose writing, while the ability to write poetically lay dormant. Then suddenly he finds he can make up a poem with a skill and originality that outfaces criticism.

We do not celebrate Patrick's achievements as an instance of precocity. There is nothing *premature* in these, any more than in Diane's. If it appears to be so, this is because the potential with which all healthy children are born is still grossly underestimated; and because human environments more often retard than advance children's ability to learn.

The all-embracing curiosity about the world which young children reveal in so marked a manner, lives or dies by the quality of each child's environment. Much of the searching, discovering, the testing, making and doing which all children need to undertake, are dependent on adult responsiveness, on the quality and appropriateness of the stimulation offered by the environment. It is our belief that only when children can be accepted and/provided for as 'prodigious learners' will they show all that they have it in them to become.

Books for Further Reading

ASHWORTH, E., *Language in the Junior School*, Edward Arnold, London.

BERNSTEIN, B. *Class, Codes and Control Volume 1: Theoretical Studies Towards a Sociology of Language*, Routledge & Kegan Paul, London and Boston (Mass.), 1971; Paladin, St Albans, 1973.

BREARLEY, M. and HITCHFIELD, E., *A Teacher's Guide to Reading Piaget*, Routledge & Kegan Paul, London, 1967; Schocken, New York, 1967.

COOPER, G. E., *The Place of Play in an Infant and Junior School*, National Froebel Foundation, London, 1958.

EGOFF, S., EGOFF, G. T. and ASHLEY, L. F., *Only Connect: Readings on Children's Literature*, Oxford University Press (Canada), Toronto, 1969.

GARDNER, D. E. M., *The Education of Young Children*, Methuen, London, 1956.

HALLIDAY, M. A. K., *Explorations on the Functions of Language*, Edward Arnold, London, 1973.

ISAACS, S., *Children and Parents: Their Problems and Difficulties* (in U.S.A., *Troubles of Children and Parents*), Routledge & Kegan Paul, London, 1968; Schocken, New York, 1973.

ISAACS, S., *Intellectual Growth in Young Children*, Routledge & Kegan Paul, London, 1930; Schocken, New York, 1966.

ISAACS, S., *The Nursery Years: The Mind of the Child from Birth to Six Years*, Routledge & Kegan Paul, London, 1932; Schocken, New York, 1968.

ISAACS, S., *Social Development in Young Children*, Routledge & Kegan Paul, London, 1933; Schocken, New York, 1972.

LABOV, W., *Language in the Inner City: Studies in the Black English Vernacular*, University of Pennsylvania Press, Philadelphia, 1973.

LEWIS, M. M., *How Children Learn to Speak*, Harrap, London, 1957.

LEWIS, M. M., *Language and the Child*, National Foundation for Educational Research, Windsor, 1969; Fernhill, New York, 1969.

LEWIS, M. M., *Language, Thought and Personality in Infancy and Childhood*, Harrap, London 1963; Basic Books, New York, 1964.

LURIA, A. R. and YUDOVICH, F. I., *Speech and the Development of Mental Processes in the Child*, Penguin Education, Harmondsworth and Baltimore, 1971.

MITCHELL, C., *Time for School: A Practical Guide for Parents of Young Children*, Penguin, Harmondsworth, 1973.

MORRIS, R., *Success and Failure in Learning to Read*, Penguin, Harmondsworth, 1973.

ROSEN, C. and ROSEN, H., *The Language of Primary School Children*, Penguin, Harmondsworth, 1973.

ROSENTHAL, R. and JACOBSON, L., *Pygmalion in the Classroom: Teacher Expectation and Pupils' Intellectual Development*, Holt, Rinehart & Winston, London and New York, 1968.

TOUGH, J., *Focus on Meaning: Talking to Some Purpose with Young Children,* Allen & Unwin, London 1974.

WINNICOTT, D. W., *The Child, the Family, and the Outside World*, Pelican, Harmondsworth and Baltimore, 1964, 1970.

YARDLEY, A., *Reaching Out* (Young Children Learning Series), Evans Brothers, London, 1970.

Index

More about Penguins
and Pelicans

Some Books on Education published in Penguin Books

Some Books on Education
published in Penguin Books